ETCHING CRAFT

Dedicated
to
Sir Frank Short, R.A., P.R.E.
in grateful acknowledgment
of his unfailing
generosity
and help

ETCHING CRAFT

A GUIDE FOR STUDENTS AND COLLECTORS

BY

W. P. ROBINS, R.E.

With a Foreword by Martin Hardie, R.E.

London : from the Office of
The Bookman's Journal & Print Collector
7 Henrietta Street, Strand, W.C. 2
1924

First Published, December 1922
Second Impression, June 1924

———

Printed in Great Britain

FOREWORD

By Martin Hardie, R.E.

(Keeper of the Department of Engraving, Illustration and Design at the Victoria and Albert Museum, South Kensington)

This brief Prologue is written with the more pleasure because for many years I have known Mr. Robins and have followed with the keenest interest and admiration the progress of his work. In our common love of Etching and our zest for the problems which it inspires, we have many a time " tired the sun with talking," while we discussed the many masters and the many methods which form the subject of the following pages. I cannot penetrate the past so far as to say that " we twa hae paidl't i' the burn," but it is certainly " lang syne "—some ten years at least—since, side by side, we dabbled in the same acid bath, breathed the same fumes, in the class of the Royal College of Art where Sir Frank Short, the supreme master-craftsman in every branch of the engraver's art, has given generous draughts to so many from the fountain of his knowledge. Ever since then, in his own practice and in teaching his students at the Central School of Arts and Crafts, Mr. Robins has gone on acquiring new knowledge and experience, and the power of imparting to others his own enthusiasm. And this kind of book, so essential to students and to collectors, can only be written by a man who is not a dilettante but a working craftsman, one who not only admires the highest art of the past, but knows why he admires it and how it was produced.

Not long ago I asked the Principal of a great School of Art what were the essentials to success in a school like his, and he replied, " A student who wants to learn;

vii

a master who knows his job and wants to teach." The author of this book knows his job. Of that there is no doubt; it is proved by his own accomplished work in the various methods about which he writes, above all by those charming dry-points which render with so much poetry and refinement the peaceful beauty of our English countryside. He wants also to teach. Of that, too, there is no doubt; or he would never have embarked on the immense labour that is involved in preparing for the press the store of facts and the helpful illustrations that this book contains. And we who want to learn—as every etcher and every lover of prints should want to learn—can find in these pages some information about what has puzzled, baffled or inspired us.

Since Sir Frank Short's book *On the Making of Etchings* went out of print many years ago, the gap caused by the want of a practical handbook has never, to my knowledge, been satisfactorily filled. Only the other day I picked up a plate of my own, which had been put aside and was badly tarnished. Nothing would remove the stains that obscured the lines; whitening and ammonia, which I thought irresistible, were of no avail. " Here at hand," thought I, " is an acid test for friend Robins," and turned to the proofs of this book which had just arrived. " Salt and vinegar," said Robins, and won my blessing. A simple and successful remedy : but just for want of a simple remedy, simply explained, the best-laid schemes of little etchers and big ones have often gone agley.

Mr. Robins, however, deals not only with the line upon line of the working etcher, but with the precept upon precept to be gained from a study of the master-etchers of the past and present. Catholic in his judgment, he can find authority and inspiration in etchers as far remote in outlook and method as Jacque and Forain, Samuel Palmer and Goya; and he wisely deals in this volume with men rather than tendencies. His book will serve a worthy purpose if it teaches the student of prints to love and choose the best, independently of origin or history or surroundings or fashion—just because it is fine work, a thing accomplished. "Tendencies," says Quiller-Couch, "did not write *The Canterbury Tales*; Geoffrey Chaucer wrote them. Influences did not make the *Faerie Queene*; Edmund Spenser made it." So we may well say: "Tendencies did not make the *Knight, Death and the Devil*; Albert Dürer wrought it. Influences did not make the *Death of the Virgin*; Rembrandt made it. Revival and tradition did not make *Le Stryge*; Meryon made it." Let us not think of etchings or mezzotints as the products of history or philosophy; let us just "praise famous men," and give up searching for abstract influences and tendencies divisible into periods and capable of being studied in compartments. If we love the highest when we see it, we need not worry about its being a superlative, with a positive and comparative, high, and higher, in the past.

And, by the same token, let us not be led away by famous names. Let us frankly recognise that the greatest masters have made only a limited number of master-pieces, and that "the man who never made a mistake never made anything." The collector should use his own judgment and not buy—or try to like—something just because it is by Rembrandt or Whistler or Haden or the latest brilliant star appearing over fashion's horizon. There are minor men—some of their names are recorded in these pages—whose work we may well respect and treasure in our portfolios, if we study not nationality or school or market prices, but the individual utterance, the individual gift. Above all, let us remember a phrase of Professor Saintsbury, that "it is not sin for a potato not to be a peach." There are potatoes and peaches in etching, and we need them both.

CONTENTS

PART IV

DRYPOINT, AQUATINT AND SOFT-GROUND ETCHINGS

PART V

PRINTING, MOUNTING, AND THE CARE OF PRINTS

PART VI

PART VII

BIBLIOGRAPHY OF WORKS ON ETCHING AND ETCHERS

LIST OF ILLUSTRATIONS

xiii

DRYPOINTS

AQUATINTS

SOFT-GROUND ETCHINGS

INTRODUCTION

INTRODUCTION

THE importance of the Graphic Arts to-day is beyond question, and the appreciation of drawings and prints seems to gather strength rather than to diminish.

The discriminating collection of drawings, etchings, lithographs and wood-engravings was never more eagerly pursued. The number of print-collectors increases astonishingly, their zest being stimulated by the informed work of numerous writers who have successfully engaged the sustained and enthusiastic interest of the lover of fine prints in achievements of the Masters of the past equally with those of the modern artist. Especially definite at the moment is the wide appreciation of etchings, not only by wealthy connoisseurs whose collections embrace the finest and rarest of prints, but also by collectors with limited means, whose discernment enables them to acquire, at a moderate price, work that will stand the test of later judgment.

Much has been written about the qualities that distinguish a fine etching, but these are best ascertained by studying closely and sympathetically the finest examples. Some knowledge of technical qualities and methods is most necessary to the would-be connoisseur, for every one of the processes by which prints are made has a definite character entirely its own, the appreciation of which should govern the formation of the collection. It is most instructive to compare fine examples in various mediums—for example, the hard brilliance of a burin

3

line with the more expressive bitten line, whether it be the free open line so insisted upon by Haden, or the rigid line of Meryon. Only by this study and comparison can the collector understand the great gulf between the beautiful deep tonal qualities of Samuel Palmer's few prints and the delicate web-like tracery of Whistler's etchings, or the sonorous strength of Brangwyn's great plates and the rich bur of an early impression in a dry-point by Muirhead Bone, to discover the fine qualities of each. In the same way will be learned the distinction between the inherent qualities of an aquatint, depending as it should on the correct relation of its bitten tones, and of a fine mezzotint wrought with subtle gradations.

To what end the modern etcher's expression is tending it is difficult to predict; certainly it has been but little affected by the recent movements that have so violently disturbed the traditions of painting.

The value of an etching as decoration is well understood to-day, for though collectors may still place their best-loved prints in solander box or portfolio, yet their treasures are much more likely to be hung upon a wall. A fine etching, in addition to the beauty of its line, will to a great extent suggest colour. Perhaps this may account for the great attraction that etching has exercised on so many fine painters who have, with a just recognition of the limitations of the medium and a correct selective faculty, frequently obtained through the etched or drypoint line a perfectly expressed individuality.

In this book I have been actuated by the desire to bring together information of use to both the collector and the student. My grateful thanks are due to Sir Frank Short, Mr. Harold Wright, Mr. Martin Hardie, Mr. Malcolm Salaman, Mr. Mark Hall, and Mr. Wilfred Partington—Founder and Editor of *The Bookman's Journal and Print Collector*—for giving me invaluable help.

My acknowledgments are due, for the loan of prints for reproduction, to those whose names appear below the plates, and to the officials of the British Museum and the Victoria and Albert Museum for assistance in many ways.

PART I

A BRIEF OUTLINE OF THE DEVELOPMENT OF ETCHING

A BRIEF OUTLINE OF THE DEVELOPMENT
OF ETCHING

THE earliest form of etching was the work of the armourers who enriched the weapons they fashioned by ornamentation bitten into the metal with acid, and from the impressions taken by pressing ink into the sunken lines and rubbing the paper with a flat tool, the process of printing etchings was discovered. Etching was at first only used as an adjunct to line engraving, and although there are prints before Rembrandt which show something of the character of the bitten line as distinct from the engraved line of the burin, it was not until the seventeenth century that Rembrandt freed the etched line from its subservience to engraving, and by the development due to his constant experiments and varying treatment of its resources, firmly established etching as a separate and entirely independent art. From his work practically the whole of etching since his time has been derived.

The first etchings were produced in Germany in the early sixteenth century, and were mostly on iron plates. The prints of Dürer, the first of the great etchers, exercised great influence in Germany, Italy, and the Netherlands.

The introduction of etching into Italy from Germany came at the time of the intense activity of the school of engravers following Marc Antonio, and the work of the artists who practised etching presents an entirely different character from the heavier German work, since

9

their line, though thinner, is much more fluent. The
early Italian etchers, however, did not advance the
technical progress of etching to any great extent.

The French etchers of the seventeenth century,
Jacques Callot (1592–1635) and Abraham Bosse (1602–
1676) both strove to imitate by etching the qualities of
engraving. Callot, a very brilliant draughtsman, covered
a wide range of subject in his prolific output, and his
line, though hard and precise, is much more interesting
than the more mechanical work of Abraham Bosse. It
was Bosse who wrote the earliest treatise on etching.
But the finest etcher of the early French School was the
great draughtsman and painter Claude Gellée (1600–
1682), who, though sometimes uncertain in his handling
of the needle and his control of the acid, produced etchings full of charm and beauty which never suggest the use
of the graver. His influence on many subsequent etchers
has been profound.

During the late sixteenth and early seventeenth
centuries there began the prolific output of etchings by
the Dutch School, these embracing the greatest variety
of subject. Figure, portrait, landscape, marine, and
animal subjects, all were essayed and treated expressively. Though the great genius of Rembrandt
exercised a powerful influence on some of his contemporaries, there were many etchers of the time who were
in no wise his imitators, and their works have an entirely
individual outlook and are essentially as Dutch as the
great master's own work.

The Italian painters exercised considerable influence
on the Dutch etchers, as they did on Dutch painting,
but the work of the Dutchmen who retained their national
outlook stands highest in the estimation of modern
criticism. In Flanders the activity of the great school
of engraving under Rubens effectually smothered every
effort to develop etching; and the consequent fate that
overwhelmed the magnificent etchings by Vandyck was

a disaster that has been lamented by generations of etchers.

Little etching was produced in the eighteenth century except in Italy and by Goya in Spain, for the popularity of line-engraving dominated everything. Of the Italian school of this period Canaletto and Tiepolo produced some magnificent etchings, and Piranesi was actively engaged in the production of his enormous plates. Fragonard in France, influenced by Tiepolo, produced some charming prints, but the finest of the eighteenth-century etchers was Goya, who bridges the great gulf between the death of Rembrandt and the advent of Meryon, and was the greatest etcher in the long interval during which line-engraving held such undisputed sway.

The influence of the etchings of Rembrandt was entirely unfelt in England until the early nineteenth century. Wenceslaus Hollar, who began the history of the English school of etching in 1637, was essentially an etcher who was governed by the tradition of line-engraving and imitated the precise line of the burin by the more easily handled needle and acid. His inimitable work, with its wide range of subject represented with wonderful decision and accuracy, left no lasting influence in England on the practice of etching as an entirely separate art. He was never influenced by the etchers of Holland. It was not until Crome, Geddes, and Wilkie revived the practice of etching in England that the Dutch influence revealed itself. Ruysdael was the inspirer of Crome's etchings as he had inspired that Norwich master's paintings. To Geddes and Wilkie, Rembrandt's etchings evidently appealed strongly.

Later in the nineteenth century came the great revival of etching in France : not since the seventeenth century had there been such a splendid group of real masters of etching. Meryon, Bracquemond, Millet, Jacque, Lalanne and Jacquemart etched many outstanding plates; the immediate result was the revival of etching in England which followed closely after with Haden, Whistler, and Palmer as its leaders, backed up by Philip Hamerton, a poor etcher but a fervent writer who helped forward the movement with the work of his critical pen. Out-standing was the work of Haden, powerful and straight-forward in its direct strength, and masterly the etchings of Whistler, whose complete command of all the resources of the medium was but slowly attained, yet consummate in those magical plates of his later period which transcend the efforts of every etcher save Rembrandt and challenge even the work of the great Dutch master. Working at the same time with Haden, Whistler, and Palmer was Legros, whose lofty style, great personality and inspired teaching had a great influence on the students whom he taught at South Kensington and the Slade School. More recently Anders Zorn, in Sweden, produced masterly portraits, some of which rank even with the work of Rembrandt and Vandyck. Of living Masters we find the fame of Sir Frank Short widespread both for his brilliant etching and for his teaching, whilst with D. Y. Cameron and Muirhead Bone—the greatest Master of drypoint since Rembrandt—the tradition of Meryon and Rembrandt is carried on. Forain, in France, has under the inspiration of Rembrandt achieved by his scriptural subjects and that splendid Lourdes series, a succession of masterpieces, while in Great Britain the prints of James McBey stand foremost among the work of younger etchers both for range of subject and brilliant expression.

PART II

THE PRACTICAL SIDE OF ETCHING

THE PRACTICAL SIDE OF ETCHING

Tools

THE methods and tools of the etcher have changed but slightly, certainly not in essentials, since the time of the early etchers. Prints by Abraham Bosse of interiors of etching workshops of the seventeenth century show in actual use the processes which we still employ to-day. The modern presses, however, with their geared action are much easier to work than the old wooden presses, but every lover of the picturesque must regret the passing of the star press with its beautiful form.

The old presses were made with wooden rollers and plank, with a four-armed star fitted directly to the top **Presses** roller, great strength being required to work them. Modern presses are all made with an iron bed on which the plate is laid when printing, and they have top and bottom rollers of steel between which the bed moves. The pressure is regulated by steel screws on each side of the press. Presses can be obtained of various sizes, from the type with fifteen-inch rollers, which is a very handy size, to the large press with forty-two inch rollers used for printing very large plates. Small bench presses are used, but they will only print small plates.

Porcelain dishes are the best, but almost any dish **Dishes** that will resist the action of acids can be used.

Any sort of steel point can be used, and in shape and size it may greatly vary; in fact, anything that will give **The Needle** a good round point, from a darning-needle set in a home-made handle to a delicate little specially-turned needle. The best way to sharpen

15

the needle is to roll it along the surface of an oilstone between the palms of the hands. (For illustrations of this and the following tools see page 17.)

This is a smooth steel tool used for reducing over-bitten lines and slight foul bitings in etching, and for **The Burnisher** modifying tones in aquatint. Etched lines are frequently over-bitten purposely to obtain the beautiful grey quality that burnished lines give. If needled and bitten correctly the etched line is the same strength throughout its length. The burnisher will reduce the line in places and give the most delicate gradations (compare Fig. 1 and Fig. 2, page 36). The tool should be very carefully looked after, for if attacked by rust it will, instead of reducing scratches, make more. It should always retain the highest polish possible. If the burnisher becomes dull and stained it can be polished with oil and crocus powder in a groove made in a piece of soft wood. A wide firewood stick is excellent for the purpose. Burnishers are made to many patterns, but the most useful shape is Fig. 12, page 17. A closely fitting leather cover is excellent to keep the burnisher in condition. Oil must be used with the tool.

The scraper is a three-edged steel tool for removing bad work, unwanted lines, or foul-biting, and should be **The Scraper** kept very sharp, the point being protected with a cork. It is also useful for removing unwanted bur from drypoint lines. A good close-grained oilstone serves to sharpen the scraper, which is continually rocked from the point upwards so as to keep the angle.

The burin, or graver, is used for line-engraving. Of steel, it is usually about four inches long and is a four-cornered or lozenge-shaped bar of steel **Burin, or Graver** ground down obliquely to the cutting end. The burin is held at a sharp angle to the plate and pushed with the palm of the hand through the metal, digging up furrows slight or deep according to

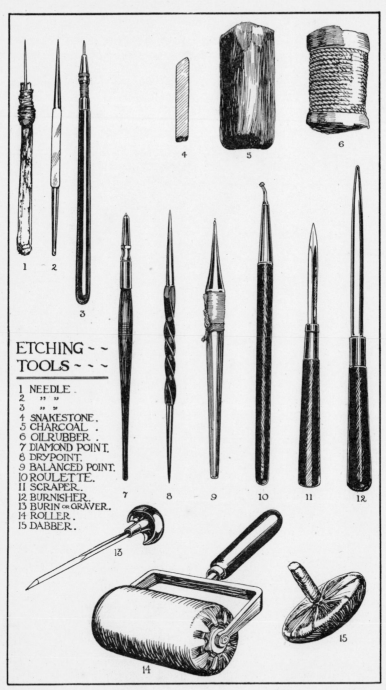

ETCHING ~~
TOOLS ~~~

1 NEEDLE .
2 ,, ,,
3 ,, ,,
4 SNAKESTONE .
5 CHARCOAL .
6 OILRUBBER .
7 DIAMOND POINT .
8 DRYPOINT .
9 BALANCED POINT .
10 ROULETTE .
11 SCRAPER .
12 BURNISHER .
13 BURIN or GRAVER .
14 ROLLER .
15 DABBER .

the strength of line needed. The plate rests on a circular sandbag and is often moved round with the left hand, the burin meanwhile being held fast with the right. The shaving of metal from the furrow made by the burin should come out cleanly, but if bur is left it can be cleared away with the scraper. The burin is often used to repair patches of badly bitten or over-burnished lines in an etching, and also in conjunction with the drypoint, as will be described later.

The hand-rest is a bridge placed over the grounded plate to avoid causing damage to the surface of the

The Hand-rest

ground by the weight and pressure of the hand during the needling. It can be made easily with a thin smooth board and two thicker supporting pieces screwed on at each end to raise the board above the surface of the plate. It is indispensable when a soft ground is used, but a good well-laid hard ground with a piece of tissue-paper over it for protection should stand the weight of the hand.

The bright surface of copper is rather dazzling to work upon and a diffused light is a great advantage. A large

The Screen

canvas stretcher, covered with strong tissue or tracing paper, and set in front of a window, makes an excellent screen. It should be hung forward at a convenient angle so as to filter the light and obviate any glare of the metal.

This is a tool which when run along the surface of the copper produces dots with a bur. The simplest form

The Roulette

is a toothed wheel, but some roulettes are made which produce irregular dots. The roulette is used with mezzotint and aquatint to repair bare places and cover slips, and it is sometimes employed with etching. Jacque used it a good deal in both his etchings and drypoints, but not always with happy results, for the character of the tool is not akin to that of the etched line and it should be used sparingly, if at all.

The oil-rubber is used for polishing the surface of the

plate. A piece of printing blanket tightly rolled and
bound round with twine makes an excellent
Oil-rubber polisher. It can be made to any dimen-
sions, but a generally useful size is two and a half inches
diameter and five inches long. A piece of compressed
felt is sometimes used. Sperm and olive are good oils for
polishing, and with a little crocus or putty powder will
give a brilliant polish to a plate.

The steel or iron plate on which grounds are laid
and plates are inked during the printing, is usually raised
on legs about six inches high to enable
The Heater a gas ring or spirit lamp to be placed
underneath.

Jigger : a wooden box with a smooth, flat top on
which inked plates are wiped during the printing; it is
usually of the same height as the heater, to
The Jigger facilitate the frequent transference of the
warm plate from the heater. It has either a lid at the top
or a flap at the side, and printing muslin and rags are
kept inside. A handy size for a jigger is eighteen inches
square.

Many varnishes can be purchased ready made. They
should dry quickly and resist the action of the acid
perfectly. Hamerton recommends a solu-
Stopping-out tion of white wax in ether and one-sixth
Varnish of Japan varnish added after the ether
solution has been decanted to clear away the sediment.
Mogul varnish and the various kinds of varnish used in
process work are all good.

Snakestone is invaluable when lines need removing
or lightening in strength. Water is used
Snakestone and the stone rubbed across the surface
of the plate. The traces of the rubbing will show on the
print and need removing from the plate, first by charcoal,
then by the oil-rubber. Snakestone can be obtained in
various sizes; broad pieces for wide work and narrow
slips for removing slight errors.

Willow charcoal is most useful when marks made by
the burnisher or scraper need removing.   It will also be
Charcoal found invaluable for reducing tones in
aquatint; oil and water are used with it.

Copper and zinc are the metals generally used for
etching upon; the invention of steel-facing has entirely
The Plate eliminated steel.   Etchers who desire to
print large editions from plates etched on
copper can, by the process of steel-facing, secure an un-
limited number of proofs by renewing the facing directly
it shows the slightest sign of wear.   Copper is most
certainly the best of all metals for etching, for it can be
worked upon with ease and certainty and can be prepared with a perfect polish and surface.   Most etchers
work upon copper such as is used for process work, and
its surface is quite good, though it is, of course, machine-
rolled and polished.   When the plate is purchased it
should be examined closely, for sometimes very undesir-
able faint lines run across the surface, and these, if they
show in the print, entail considerable trouble to remove
satisfactorily.   Hammered copper is more expensive but
much preferable, especially for mezzotint or drypoint.
The hardness of the hammered plate is a great advantage,
and the added quality and even density imparted by the
hammering make the plate much more sympathetic to
work upon.

Plates can be re-faced by the old work being planed
off and the new surface repolished, and if old hammered
plates are secured they can be re-faced over and over
again.

Zinc is also largely used, though with zinc the action
of the acid is more rapid and the bitten line is somewhat
coarser than that given by copper.   It is also much
softer than copper and will not print so large an edition
if the lines are bitten delicately.

Preparation of the Plate

A bevelled edge to the plate is very essential, for without it the plate under the pressure of the rollers of the press will cut through the paper and sometimes cut and ruin the blankets. This bevel makes the so-called plate-mark. If the bevelling is not done before the plate is purchased, a rough file will quickly remove the amount of copper necessary. Care has to be taken to secure the plate firmly during the filing, or the file will slip and gash the surface of the plate. The filings are brushed off the surface of the plate with a large soft brush, not with a rag. A smooth bevel is obtained by using a finer file and finishing with a burnisher. When a rough bevel is left the edge of the plate will print much darker than the plain surface of the copper, giving a rather unsightly effect to the print.

The best method of cleaning the plate, to remove any traces of grease from the surface before the ground **Cleaning the Plate** is laid, is to rub the plate gently but thoroughly with a piece of perfectly clean rag soaked in a paste made with finely ground whitening mixed with water and a fair proportion of ammonia. Ordinary whitening is too gritty and will often produce scratches. The paste should be washed off under a tap, and if the water will run freely anywhere on the plate, it should be safe to lay the ground. The plate should now be dried and wiped with a clean rag, and, throughout the cleaning, and while laying the ground, it should be handled as carefully as a photographic plate, the surface never being touched by the fingers.

The ground is the thin coating of wax which protects the plate from the action of the acid and through which **The Ground** the etcher scratches with his needle the lines he intends to bite into the metal. Very good grounds can be purchased ready-made, but it is very desirable to know both the constituents and the

21

preparation.   The necessary qualities of the ground are
a sufficient degree of adhesiveness to ensure that it will
hold firmly to the plate, that it is not too hard, and
therefore will not flake or chip off when the needle is
used, and lastly—and most important—that it will resist
perfectly the various mordants used to bite the lines.
Most grounds are made with varying combinations of
white wax, gum mastic, and asphaltum, and sometimes
pitch is added.   Hamerton recommends Abraham Bosse's
ground, which consists of pure white wax 50 grammes,
gum mastic 30 grammes, asphaltum 15 grammes.   Sir
Frank Short gives this recipe which makes a perfect
hard ground : pure beeswax 2½ oz., Syrian asphaltum
2 oz., Burgundy pitch ½ oz., black pitch ½ oz.   The pitch
gives a greater degree of adhesiveness.   A slightly larger
amount of wax will give a little softer ground more suit-
able for a cold atmosphere.   To prepare the ground, the
wax is melted first in a perfectly clean china pot, or large
jam-pot, placed in water in a saucepan, and the gum
mastic or pitch, very finely powdered, is then slowly
added to the melted wax.   The mixture is continually
stirred with a glass rod, the asphaltum, also finely
ground, being added last.   After simmering gently for
from fifteen to twenty minutes, the ground is poured
into lukewarm water and rolled into short sticks or balls.
The hands should be thoroughly wetted before the
rolling is commenced.

The method most commonly used for laying grounds
is by the dabber.   The dabber (see page 17) is composed
of a wad of cotton wool placed upon a disc
Laying the   of cardboard, with a piece of silk or kid
Ground   drawn tightly across the wool, and bound
with cotton at the back of the disc.   A handle of some
sort is necessary; a wooden one may be bound on or
the spare silk or kid utilised for the purpose.   Great care
needs to be taken to keep the surface of the dabber
clean; it is impossible to lay a good ground with a dirty

or hard dabber. If the dabber—which will last a long
time if properly used and kept in a box—becomes charged
with too much ground, it can be cleaned by warming it
upon the heater and rubbing the overcharged covering
with some printing muslin. The plate is next placed
upon the heater, which must be kept at an even temperature warm enough to melt the wax when it is rubbed
gently on to the surface of the plate. Care must be taken
not to burn the ground. It will be impossible to etch
upon if burnt, for it will be found defective either when
needling or during the biting. Just sufficient ground is
melted to cover thinly the whole of the plate, and it is
spread over the surface with a small piece of perfectly
clean printing muslin. The plate is now dabbed quickly
all over until it is covered with a thin and perfectly even
coat of the ground. Thin grounds work much better
than thicker ones, and the usual fault with students
laying grounds is to make them much too thick. The
etching ground can be laid with a roller (see page 17),
but the heat soon hardens the roller. The leather-
covered roller is the best for this purpose and it needs to
be cleaned immediately after use.

While the plate is still warm a hand-vice is fastened
on to a selected place, chosen where it will least interfere
with the needling, and the plate held face
Smoking the Ground downwards over a bundle of lighted tapers
or a gas smoker (see page 24). The smoke
changes the brown wax to a jet black, enabling the etcher
to see clearly every mark made by his needle and, if he
wishes to trace his design, giving a perfect surface to
receive the tracing of the drawing from which the etching
is to be made. The plate is passed slowly backwards
and forwards above the flame, care being taken not to
burn the ground, which would then tend to break off in
flakes. Grey patches upon the ground after the plate
has been smoked show that the ground is burnt and needs
to be cleaned off and laid again.

SMOKING THE GROUND
(See previous page)

The subject may be drawn direct on the plate from nature, though the print will then be in reverse. If **Tracing and Transferring** made from a drawing the work on the plate will also, when printed, show the drawing in reverse. To overcome this difficulty a looking-glass is used and the drawing propped up, and the etching worked from the reflection in the glass. If it is desired to get the print as near as possible to the design, a tracing made with a soft pencil on thin tracing (not greasy) paper should be transferred on to the ground. After a tracing is completed and cut to the size of the plate, the tracing paper is slightly damped and laid pencil side down to the smoked ground and passed through the press just as a proof would be taken. The pencil lines will appear quite plainly on the smoked ground in grey lines. The pressure does not require to be as great as for printing a proof or the paper will stick to the plate and ruin tracing and ground alike. If the pressure is not altered with the key, one of the blankets should be taken out. This transfer can be fused into the ground by gently heating the plate so that it will

not rub off. Without a press the best way to transfer
the drawing to the plate is to use red transfer-paper.   A
tracing of the drawing is made, reversed, and pinned
down over the transfer-paper upon the plate and the
lines run over with a pencil or stylus.   The outline of the
design can also be sketched on the ground with thin
Chinese white.

The roller, covered with either leather or indiarubber,
lays a very fine ground, thin and very clear; and the
Rolled Paste Grounds only drawback to its use is that it cannot
be worked upon immediately, for the spike
oil of lavender takes some time to evapor-
ate, and it is as well to allow at least twenty-four hours
to elapse before using the grounded plate.   One oz. of
ordinary ground is dissolved into a paste by melting it
with 2 oz. of spike oil of lavender.   The ground is broken
up, placed into a wide-mouthed bottle with the oil of
lavender, and the bottle put into a tin or saucepan of
water and gently heated until the ground is melted.
The bottle is kept tightly corked and a little spike oil
is added if the paste becomes too hard.   To lay the
ground a little of the paste is taken out of the bottle
with a small palette knife and spread over a piece of
glass; the roller is then run backwards and forwards
over the paste until the former is evenly covered.   The
roller is next rolled across the plate in every direction
until the surface is evenly covered with a thin coating of
the ground.   The plate is then gently heated and smoked.
The roller must always be cleaned with printing muslin
and the palm of the hand.

Liquid grounds composed of 1 oz. ordinary ground
dissolved in 4 oz. of chloroform or ether are largely used,
Liquid Grounds and though it is perhaps more difficult for
the novice to get a perfect ground by this
method, a little experience will enable him
to coat a plate with a very smooth ground excellent to
work upon.   For small or moderate-sized plates the

solution is poured over the centre of the plate, and the
entire surface is covered by gently tilting the plate.   No
more liquid is used than is necessary to cover the whole
surface, and the superfluous amount can be poured back
into the bottle from one of the corners.   The chloroform
or ether will evaporate very quickly, and the plate is
warmed upon the heater until the surface shines, then it
is smoked in the ordinary way.   Larger plates are coated
in a shallow bath which needs to be slightly tilted.   The
plate is covered as rapidly as possible, taken out of the
bath and allowed to dry.   Quickness and deftness in
handling the plate are the chief things to aim for when
laying liquid grounds.   Dust is the enemy of all grounds,
but especially of liquid grounds, and early morning is
the best time for this work.   Liquid grounds are apt
to chip off in cold weather and are often rather too
thick.

Transparent ground, made without pitch or asphaltum,
is often used when additional work is required to
Transparent Ground complete a plate.   The previously bitten
lines can be clearly seen, and the only slight
difficulty with the method is that the new
needling is somewhat difficult to follow until the biting
commences. Transparent ground is not so safe as
ordinary ground and foul biting often occurs when it is
used, and all the parts of the plate not being needled are
painted over with stopping-out varnish.

The back and the edges of the plate must always be
coated with the stopping-out varnish to protect them
from the action of the acid.   If the plate is put into the
bath before this is done the large expanse of metal being
attacked will often cause such violent biting that the
plate itself will move about in the bath.   The edges if
unprotected will be bitten very roughly, and when
the plate is printed will give a very unpleasant
border.

Great care needs to be taken to penetrate the ground,

for if the copper is not fully exposed unequal biting will

Needling
occur.   It is better to use too much pressure than too little.   The needle is held as upright as possible and it works freely if the point be correctly sharpened with a perfectly round point.

BITING THE PLATE

For the way to perfection is through a series of disgusts.—
PATER.

Nothing is more trying to the temper of the etcher than the uncertainty of the action of his mordant, *i. e.* the acid used to bite into the metal the lines drawn through the wax ground.   Even years of experience will not eliminate the hazard of the process.   The novice by good luck may bite his first plate with perfect success, though he may never repeat the performance; and the etcher of long experience may overbite or underbite. The acid most commonly used is nitric; all acids should always be kept in glass-stoppered bottles.

A safe working proportion is three parts of nitric acid of a specific gravity of 1·42 to five parts of water,

Nitric Bath
though frequently a mixture is used as strong as half acid and half water.   If the bath is diluted the lines will be finer, but the biting will take much longer.   Strong nitric baths will broaden and roughen the line.   For illustrations of various bitings with the nitric bath see page 28.   Bubbles of gas arise from the action of the acid in the line, and these are a good guide to the progress of the biting and need to be watched closely.   Any lines that are not biting will show no bubbles, and the plate is taken out, washed, and the lines reworked.   A feather can be used to wipe off the bubbles directly they show plainly; if they are allowed to remain, unequal biting will result, and they are always brushed away.

A freshly mixed bath is never used.   When the bath is made up it is poured into a dish and some scrap copper put into it, even if it necessitates the illegal act of dissolving a copper coin when no scrap copper is available. The bath when finished with is filtered to eliminate scraps of stopping-out varnish which may have fallen from the back of the plate and the various impurities which get into the liquid from other causes. If these

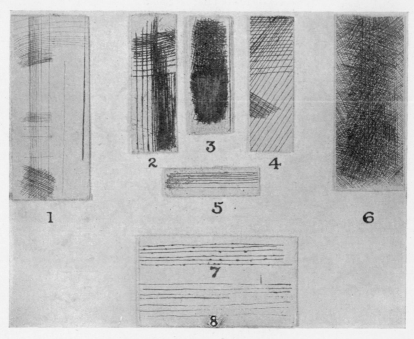

NITRIC BATH EXAMPLES.

No. 1. Lines bitten for 15 minutes in weak Nitric, 1 of acid to 2 of water, showing the effect of the acid on the closely needled work.

No. 2. Lines bitten for 5 minutes in strong Nitric, 3 of acid to 2 of water.

No. 3. Lines at top were bitten for 15 minutes in Nitric (3 of acid to 5 of water) and then stopped out. The lower part of the plate was bitten for a further 15 minutes, with the result that the work broke up.

No. 4. Lines bitten for 10 minutes in Nitric, 3 of acid to 5 of water.

No. 5. Lines bitten for 30 seconds only in pure Nitric, brushed on with a feather.

No. 6. Example of cross-hatching obtained by adding lines as the biting progressed.

No. 7. Example of pitting.

No. 8. Example of rotten lines.

are allowed to remain they cloud the work and make it difficult to see what is happening to the plate during the biting. The nitric bath requires strengthening occasion-

ally with new acid.   The fumes given off from the bath
are not dangerous, but reasonable care is always taken
not to inhale the fumes unnecessarily.   Acids are always
handled carefully and the bottles never grasped by the neck.

Another bath frequently used is the Dutch mordant,
which is composed of chlorate of potash 20 grammes,
hydrochloric acid 100 grammes, water 880
grammes.   The chlorate of potash is dissolved in hot, not boiling, water, well stirred,
and when the crystals are entirely gone the mixture is
left to cool and the acid added.   The Dutch mordant
bites deeper than the nitric bath, but does not enlarge

The Dutch Bath

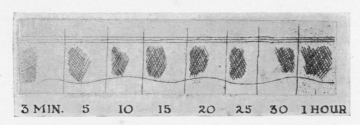

DUTCH BATH EXAMPLES.

the line so much and attacks the metal much more
regularly than the nitric bath.   It is kept at a temperature of between 75 and 85° F. when the biting is
proceeding, and a piece of sheet asbestos beneath the
dish on the heater is necessary, with the gas or spirit
stove turned low.   The Dutch bath when it is first
poured out into the dish gives off chlorine gas; it is
therefore advisable to wait a few minutes before leaning
over the dish.   When biting very deeply with the
Dutch bath, it is as well, now and then, to dip the plate
(after well washing it) into the nitric bath; this will
clear a film which is deposited on the bitten surface.

It is often of great advantage to use both the Dutch
and the nitric baths in biting a plate, so obtaining the contrast of the delicate wiry line given by the Dutch bath,
with the rougher wider line obtained with the nitric.

The work might be commenced in the Dutch bath, and, after the more delicate lines are bitten, the plate should be washed very thoroughly under the water-tap to ensure that the acids are not mixed, and after the plate is dried any work that is sufficiently bitten should be stopped out. The plate may then be placed in the nitric bath and remaining work finished with the rougher quality of the nitric line.

A third bath which is frequently used is perchloride of iron, which makes a splendid mordant. It bites a deep clear line, and the only fault in its use **Perchloride of Iron Bath** is the dark colour which makes it rather difficult to judge how the biting is progressing. Perchloride of iron can be procured either in a liquid form or in powder.

When the whole, or almost the whole, of the work has been needled on the plate before it is placed in the **Stopping-out** bath, it is necessary during the process of the biting to use stopping-out varnish to obtain difference in the strength of the lines. After the plate has been bitten sufficiently for the lightest passages to tell correctly, it is taken out of the bath, washed well with water and thoroughly dried with blotting-paper. The lines which are intended to remain light are then covered over with the varnish, which dries fairly quickly, and if painted on correctly the varnish will stop the acid from attacking these lines again. The varnish should not be too thin, as otherwise it would have a tendency to run down and fill the lines adjacent to those stopped out. It were better to be a little thick to avoid any danger of spreading. When the varnish is quite dry, the plate is again immersed in the bath and the second biting completed, which causes all the lines left exposed to be strengthened. The remaining work is bitten and portions are successively stopped out until finally only the darkest and heaviest lines are left to be bitten.

It will be realised that this process of stopping-out,

though simple when the etching consists of a few open lines with no great amount of detail, becomes extremely difficult when very complicated needling is used, such as cross-hatching, or where lighter lines are wanted across heavier work. This difficulty may be overcome by altering the entire procedure and by not using the stopping-out varnish at all. Only the darkest and strongest lines wanted are needled first and bitten. The plate is then washed and dried, and the lighter lines added and bitten; the process is continued until all the finer details of the work are needled and bitten. With this method good judgment is needed to regulate the difference in the bitings, but with ordinary care it is not difficult to obtain a good result.

Another method of biting is that in which the work is needled while the plate is in the bath, and with experience this method is easily controlled. The action of the acid is at once apparent and the trouble of lines not biting because the ground is not exposed by the needle is avoided. The needle is, of course, bitten away by the acid, but retains its sharpness. The darkest lines are needled first, and the whole etching completed by adding the lighter work, while the plate is still in the acid. The necessity of stopping-out is thus avoided and a perfect gradation of strength of line obtained.

Care should be taken in all cases to detect foul biting (see Fig. 3, page 35). If it is suspected that this is occurring, a little of the ground is taken off the surface and the plate examined. This can easily be done with a thin brush and a little turpentine, any suspicious places being painted out with stopping-varnish. In a warm room the action of all the baths is much faster than in a cold atmosphere. For instance, if the nitric bath is warmed over the heater it will at once attack the copper and begin to bubble very hard. Sometimes this rapid biting is useful. Open work with the lines well apart bites very much more slowly than closely needled work. This can be seen in Fig. 1, page 28. Very great care must be taken with biting very close work, for the acid attacking the copper underneath the ground causes the fine work to break away, and the result in the print is a grey unpleasant tone instead of a number of close lines. See Fig. 3 on page 28, in which the lines at the top were bitten for fifteen minutes and then stopped out. The additional biting for fifteen minutes caused the rest of the work to break up.

Zinc plates are bitten in a nitric bath with a strength much less than for copper; the best proportion is 1 of acid to 7 of water.

Judging the depth of the lines while the biting is progressing is a great trouble to the student, who at first will be hopelessly at sea; his most certain method is to take a fine brush dipped in turpentine and remove a small portion of the ground. Later, with more experience, the feel of the lines if the needle is run along them will tell how deeply they are bitten.

The biting being now completed, the plate is washed and dried, placed upon the heater and warmed, and the ground on the front, and the varnish on the back are cleaned off with turpentine and a rag. Here some restraint is necessary in the natural anxiety to see the result of the biting. The varnish on the back of the plate is cleaned off before the ground on the front, as the face of the plate has to be protected as much as possible or it may become scratched.

It is often found when the first proof from the plate has been taken that portions, or even the whole, of the **Re-biting** etching are underbitten. In this case a re-biting ground is laid and the same lines bitten again to the desired depth. The process is a delicate one and very great care has to be taken to avoid foul-biting. The plate is very carefully cleaned and some re-biting ground—ordinary dark ground mixed into a paste with spike oil of lavender—placed upon a piece of glass. A leather-covered roller is next passed backwards and forwards over the plate on the glass until it is charged with a thin even covering of the paste. The roller is then run lightly over the plate with very little pressure until the whole surface of the plate is covered with the ground. The very greatest care has to be taken not to press the ground into the lines, for that will, of course, prevent the acid from biting again. The plate is now very gently heated to expel the spike oil. Smoking the ground is unwise, for the delicate shallow lines are almost sure to fill. If possible the plate is left for two days and the spike oil allowed to evaporate naturally. To ensure that the ground is not pressed by the roller into the lines they are often filled with a paste of whitening, which is allowed to dry thoroughly before the ground is laid. Care needs to be taken to see that the whitening is wiped away from the surface of the plate and only allowed to remain in the lines. Re-biting is a hazardous business and requires to be used sparingly, as the work almost always loses its freshness and, however carefully the ground is laid, some of the delicate lines are almost certain to be filled, when uneven biting results.

If the first proof from the plate shows that additional work is necessary a re-working ground has to be laid. The ground is laid either with the dabber **Re-working** or the roller, but it is imperative that all the previously bitten lines be filled. More often than not the edges of the old lines will re-bite when the plate is in the bath for the re-working, and the best way to avoid this trouble is to warm the plate on the heater and with a piece of clean muslin drive the ground well into the lines. The surface of the plate is then wiped as clean as possible with printing muslin and the plate is allowed to cool. When the plate is quite cold a rolled paste ground can be laid over both the filled lines and the surface of the plate. The new lines can then be

D

needled and the plate bitten with no anxiety as to the
old work biting again. The plate may be re-grounded and
bitten as many times as are necessary to complete the
etching.

FAULTS

Pitting is a fault that often occurs, and is caused by
impurities in the ground.   The line prints with spots
            dotted along its length, rather like the
Pitting   floats on a seine net.   I have imitated it
in Fig. 7, page 28.   Pitting is easily perceived when
the nitric bath is being used, for the spots on lines show
clearly and are detected at once.   With the Dutch
mordant these are much more difficult to detect, owing
to the darkening of the lines during the biting.   Directly
the lines show signs of pitting, the plate is taken out and
washed well and, with a very fine brush, the affected places
are stopped out.   If perceived in time they will be found
to be very slightly bitten and can be easily removed, the
lines being afterwards repaired with the burin or drypoint.

Rotten lines are caused by unequal biting due to the
ground not having been equally removed by an even
            pressure of the needle, for the tendency
Rotten Lines of the beginner is to work as with a
pencil, with increasing pressure here and there to give
variety or emphasis.   On those parts of the line where
the needle has only partially gone through the ground,
the action of the acid is delayed through the thin film
of ground left by the needle protecting the copper there,
while the fully exposed parts of the line are biting correctly.   Sometimes there are even gaps in the line which
will be found not to have bitten at all.   I have endeavoured
to show this in Fig. 8, page 28.   These can be re-touched
with the drypoint if the lines are light, or with the burin,
but correct needling with an even pressure will obviate
the necessity of tinkering with the lines in this fashion.

FIG. 1. See page 37.

FIG. 2. See page 38.

FIG. 3. See page 38.

FIG. 4. See page 38.

FAULTS AND CORRECTIONS.

FIG. 1. See page 38.

FIG. 2. See page 39.

FIG. 3. See page 39.

FIG. 4. See page 39.

FAULTS AND CORRECTIONS.

The little plates reproduced on pages 35 and 36 were etched to show examples of many of the pitfalls that **Further Faults** await the etcher. Some of these pitfalls are avoidable if average care be taken; others will plague the experienced etcher as much as the novice.

Fig. I, page 35.—The scratches across the plate might be caused by badly ground ink, or by grit on the printing muslin, or even through using gritty whitening before the ground is laid. If the printing muslin happens to drop on the floor it should be thrown away at once. Scratches are a great trial and nuisance to etchers, particularly when they occur on the more delicate parts of the work, and it needs great care to remove them successfully. A frequent cause of scratches is that the rag has accidentally picked up some of the tiny filings or scrapings from the bench. Sometimes a filing will get on to the face of the oil-rubber and produce, during the polishing, scores of scratches, which is heartrending when delicate work happens to be underneath. The scratches on the plate here reproduced were removed by first scraping very lightly along the length of the scratch, then the burnisher was pressed diagonally across the line left after this scraping, with an even pressure forcing the sides of the line together, and closing them up so that when printed it held no ink; finally the plate was polished with the oil-rubber and a little putty powder and oil. The over-bitten patch on the cheek was first scraped and then hammered up from the back. This hammering is a simple and effective way of removing such faults. With a pair of callipers specially made for the task, the place corresponding to the fault on the back of the plate was gently hammered with a punch until the pit or depression on the face of the plate was brought level with the rest of the surface. Care had to be taken to find the exact spot to punch and to ensure that too much force was not used for fear a bump should be raised on the face of the plate which would show in the print. After the hammering, the spot was lightly burnished and then polished with the oil-rubber and putty-powder. The two small patches of slightly over-bitten lines below the collar were lightly burnished and polished with the finger and a little oil. Fig. 2, page 35, shows the print after the removal of the faults.

Fig. 3, page 35.—This little plate is an example of very bad foul biting. Such extensive fouling might be caused by a very badly laid ground or by burning during the smoking. In this case it was due to the plate not being properly freed from grease. Of course, if the bath used is nitric acid, fouling of this nature is quickly noticed because of the bubbles which form very thickly on such portions. If the Dutch mordant is used, it is more difficult to detect fouling, and such accidents as happened to the sky in our little plate might occasionally occur. The whole surface of the sky and the patch over the bank of the stream in the left corner were first strongly scraped. The rick was then lightly scraped and the heaviest spots remaining hammered up. The marks of the scraper were removed by rubbing with snakestone and water. Willow charcoal and oil were then used to remove the marks of the snakestone, and after that the plate was rubbed with fine emery paper, and the final polish given by the oil-rubber and putty-powder. A second ground was then laid and the plate reworked and completed (see Fig. 4, page 35).

A vice is very useful in such operations as the above, for if the plate is clamped to a bench or table, scraping, snakestoning and polishing can be managed with much greater ease. A small pad should cover the head of the vice where it grips the plate, or heavy marks will be caused such as are seen on the right lower corner of Fig. 1, page 36. In this plate the sky and distance were over-bitten and had to be burnished down and polished with the oil-rubber, no charcoal being used. A little drypoint was added to the tree and the bur was removed with the scraper, the result of these corrections being shown in Fig. 2, page 36.

Fig. 3, page 36, shows a print from a plate which was under-bitten and found to need further work. A new ground was laid over the old work and additional lines added, but the plate was forgotten and left in the bath for an hour, with the result seen in Fig. 4, page 36.

Carelessness in handling and storing will often cause the surface of plates to tarnish. Students have been **Stains** known to wrap their plates in blotting-paper which has been used for drying plates after they have been bitten in the acid bath. The usual result of such treatment is almost certain ruin to any delicate work, and entails a lot of laborious work to repair the damage. The best way to carry plates is to wrap them in tissue-paper, or, better still, in a flannel-lined case, and grounded plates can be carried without damage pinned down upon the boards in a slotted box. Damp is a great cause of stains on copper, and if steel-faced plates are left exposed they will quickly be ruined, for the damp eats into them. Plates should always be kept in a dry place and covered with a protective coating of beeswax or hard ground. A solution of common salt and vinegar will remove most slight stains from copper, and a quick short immersion in a very diluted nitric bath will often clean a plate. Putty-powder and the oil-rubber will polish most superficial stains from a bitten plate, but a drypoint should only be rubbed lightly with a soft rag soaked with the vinegar and salt solution. To use the oil-rubber on a drypoint is fatal, for not only will the bur be damaged, but the plate in all probability will be badly scratched. If there are stains on a plain surface of the drypoint plate, use the oil and putty powder, and polish, with felt round the finger.

Note.—All the technical illustrations to this and other Parts necessarily suffer in reproduction, but it is hoped that, in conjunction with the text, they demonstrate the points made.

PART III

THE GREAT ETCHERS AND THEIR WORK

THE GREAT ETCHERS AND THEIR WORK

EARLY GERMAN SCHOOL

IN this chapter the development of etching is shown in outline from the earliest prints of the German school to the work of the modern Master-etchers. The notes on the artists and the reproductions of their work have been designed to give, as far as possible, a concise view of the successive schools and also to serve as a guide to the study required for a complete knowledge and appreciation of the art of etching.

Urs. Graf, about 1485–1529 Urs Graf, a Swiss engraver, produced the earliest known etching in about 1513, and the prints of Dürer etched on iron plates were made about the same time.

Daniel Hopfer, about 1493–1536 Hopfer etched a great number of designs for gold-smiths' ornaments. He was probably the first German to etch in the modern sense of the term. His work was mainly of a reproductive tendency.

Albrecht Dürer, 1471–1528 Dürer's plates were bitten with a very even line and display a fine austerity of style and lofty imagination. Dürer was essentially an engraver, and he never appears to have realised the possibility of developing the character of the bitten line, with its greater freedom, in a distinctive manner. His etchings, although more open in treatment than his line engravings, have a character much more akin to his glorious woodcuts. His etching, *Angels with the Emblems of Passion*, is a splendid print with a fine effect of light on the figure of the angel and the breaking clouds. *The Cannon* is a wonderfully drawn landscape with the great expanse of country stretching to the hills, which are thrown into fine relief by the darker sky

43

behind them. *The Agony in the Garden* (see page 45), etched with a very powerful line, has all the great qualities of design and draughtsmanship that make Dürer's engravings so completely distinctive.

Among the earliest etchers of the German school was Hans Sebald Beham. This skilful en-
Hans Beham, 1500–1550 graver etched decorative subjects, of which *The Fool and the Lady*, and *A Soldier*, are examples.

Albrecht Altdorfer, a follower of Dürer's manner, pro-
Altdorfer, abt. 1480–1538 duced some etched landscapes and a number of etchings of jewellers' cups.

Hirschvogel was one of the earliest etchers to produce prints that really differed in character from line
Augustin Hirschvogel, 1503–1553 engravings. They sometimes have a sensitive, suggestive line and delicacy of treatment that is surprising. *Houses by a River*, and the small long plate with the Rocks and Castles exemplify these qualities.

Hans Sebald Lautensack, another etcher of this early
Lautensack, 1524–abt. 1563 German period, whose work is much more involved in treatment than Hirschvogel's.

Burgkmair etched decorative designs. The coat of arms
Hans Burgkmair the Younger, 1530–1560 of Augsburg is an example. The original iron plate of his etching, *Mercury and Venus*, may be seen in the British Museum.

Other early German etchers were Jost Amman (1539–1591), who etched decorative works and portraits, and Virgil Solis (1514–1562), whose portrait of *Johannes Gemel* is noteworthy.

ITALIAN ETCHERS, SIXTEENTH AND SEVENTEENTH CENTURIES

The introduction of etching into Italy was of later
Francisco Mazzuoli, called Parmigiano, 1503–1540 date than in Germany, the discovery being taken into Italy and first practised by Parmigiano, who etched about 1525. The

ALBRECHT DÜRER: *The Agony in the Garden*. Etching,
1st state (B. 19); size of original, 8¾″ × 6⅛″.

From a print in the British Museum.

JAN VAN DE VELDE: *March*, from the series of Months. Etching; size of original, $6\frac{1}{4}'' \times 8\frac{3}{4}''$.

From a print in the British Museum.

fluent composition of his drawings is reflected in his etchings, of which *The Resurrection* and *Judith* are good examples.

Meldolla, a follower of Parmigiano, etched with a free

Andrea Schiavone Meldolla, 1522–1582 style, and also used drypoint. The print *Minerva and the Muses* is a good example of his work.

Barocci etched with a just perception of the resources

Barocci of Urbino, 1528–1612 of the medium. The large plate *The Annunciation*, is a good example, and the smaller plate *Vision of St. Francis* has interesting qualities.

Guido Reni, a famous painter, etched some very good

Guido Reni, 1575–1642 plates. *The Virgin and Child* and *The Infant Christ and St. John* are examples.

The painter Ribera, working in Italy, was the first of

Jose Ribera, 1588–1652 the Spanish school to etch, and his line is strong and expressive. The *St. Jerome* and the *Satyr and Silenus* are good plates.

There are only two etchings by the painter, Guercino,

Guercino, 1591–1666 the *St. John the Baptist* and *St. Anthony of Padua*. The latter is a graceful design and a well-treated plate.

The Neapolitan artist, Salvator Rosa, etched with a

Salvator Rosa, 1615–1673 lively, suggestive line scenes of the military life of his time.

Castiglione was a contemporary of Salvator Rosa

Castiglione, 1616–1670 who was strongly influenced by Rembrandt and Van Dyck.

Della Bella followed Callot's manner closely. *La*

Stefano Della Bella, 1610–1664 *Place Dauphine, du Côte du Pont Neuf* is a characteristic example.

EARLY DUTCH SCHOOL

Among the earliest of the Dutch school of etchers was

Jan Van de Velde, 1593–1641 Jan Van de Velde, who produced landscapes and figure subjects. The set, *Seasons*, shows his precise manner, but he reveals little perception of the distinctive quality of the etched line. *Summer* is an example of his formal design, with the great mill towering over the trees in the foreground and the finely drawn distance. The plate has a variety of human interest very expressively drawn. In the print *March* (page 46) from the series called *The Months*, the effect of the wind sweeping over the country is admirably caught.

Some delicately bitten costume studies charmingly placed on the plates were produced by Buytenwegh, whose **William** manner somewhat resembles the French-**Buytenwegh,** man Callot. *The Dutch Nobleman* is a **1590–1630** delightful example in which the head expresses a very whimsical character.

The prints of Seghers are particularly interesting to the student, for they show the first attempts and experiments with colour-printing from **Hercules Seghers,** copper plates. His etchings, though some-**1590–1645** what intricate, show an effort to express nature faithfully and have often a very poetic quality. Rembrandt altered one of Seghers' landscapes, the *Tobias and the Angel*, and after removing the large figures at the right of the plate, replaced them with the Holy Family, and renamed the plate *The Flight into Egypt* (H. 266). The *Landscape with a River* is a treatment of an immense flat expanse of country such as Phillipe Koninck painted later; the planes are perfectly suggested and the detail is well handled. Seghers' rendering of wooded scenes, though very elaborately worked, is very good. The *Landscape with a Road through a Wood* represents this side of his etched work admirably.

The work of Molyn (I) is exceedingly interesting, for, though his line is somewhat hard, yet his conception of landscape etching is very near to Rem-**Pieter Molyn (I),** brandt's. The print reproduced, *Landscape* **1595–1661** *with Tree and Ruined Cottage* (page 49), has a quiet intimate simplicity, and while perhaps not

PIETER MOLYN I : *Landscape with a Tree and Ruined Cottage.* Etching ; size of
original, 5″ × 6½″.

From a print in the British Museum.   49
    E

PETRVS BREVGEL
ANTVERPIÆ PICTOR RVRALIVM ACTIONVM.

Ant. van Dyck fecit aqua forti

SIR ANTHONY VAN DYCK: *Pieter Breughel.* Etching
(B. 2); size of original, $9\frac{1}{2}'' \times 6\frac{1}{4}''$.

50   From a print in the collection of Mr. Harold J. L. Wright.

so free in style as the print, *Man and Woman in a Land-scape*, yet its qualities of design are unpretentious and entirely free from the German influence. *The Travellers* is another characteristic etching by Molyn.

The Early Flemish School

Van Leyden executed a portrait of the Emperor Maxi-
Lucas Van Leyden, milian I in 1520 which is largely etching,
1494–1533 though the burin governs the treatment of the line.

While the activity of Rubens was almost entirely
Peter Paul Rubens, directed to the school of engraving which
1577–1640 he founded, he is reputed to have etched the print called *St. Catherine.*

The one great etcher of the Flemish school was Van Dyck, whose etched portraits form an important land-
Sir Anthony mark in the history of etching. These
Van Dyck, prints were executed in a spirit entirely
1599–1641 at variance with the engraved work of his time, and though they were quite unappreciated and were finished with the addition of backgrounds engraved by other hands with the burin, yet the earlier states have been an inspiration for succeeding generations of etchers. The portrait of *Pieter Breughel* (page 50) well represents the Flemish master with its massive character-isation, economy of line, and virile drawing. *Lucas Vorsterman* is a strongly bitten plate with a fine sugges-tion of rich colour, the portrait of the truculent engraver being a great contrast in treatment to the justly famed self-portrait of Van Dyck, which is much more delicately etched, with very simple lighting. The grave head of *Franz Snyders,* the still-life painter, is beautifully drawn, and *Adam van Noort,* with his more homely features, wonderfully depicted, is another splendid example of the famous series. In the etching of *Antonie Cornelissen,* the poise of the head on the bulky shoulders is admirable.

The Early French School

Of the earliest French etchers Callot was the most prolific. He advanced the technique of etching by re-

Jacques Callot, 1592–1635

working his plates after the first state, and produced more than a thousand prints. Greatly varied in subject, their manner is akin to engraving. They are very cleanly printed and well display his vigorous, observant draughtsmanship. *The Seven Deadly Sins* are a fine set of plates, especially the *Envy*, and the dramatic and forcible set, *The Miseries of War*, show Callot's power in its widest range. His portraits are in line very like engraving, and the series of his records of contemporary costumes are very interesting. He etched a number of studies of Beggars which are full of character, closely studied, and well recorded. Of these the print reproduced (page 53) is a good example.

Mr. J. Pennell in a recently published book of lectures given at Chicago, while paying tribute to Claude's power

Claude Gellée, 1600–1682

as a draughtsman, says : " He too was forced to etch, and he etched vilely." *Le Bouvier* (page 54) is hardly a " vile etching." Granted that it does not conform to the limitations within which Mr. Pennell would circumscribe etching, yet *Le Bouvier* is a print of poetic power that will always compel the admiration of the discerning connoisseur and student. Claude's prints have had great influence on modern landscape etching. He was the first lyrical etcher, and all his work is full of light. The *Cattle Going Home in Stormy Weather* is a lovely print with a delicately suggested sky and play of shadow across the spacious hilly country, the light just catching the large tower on the wooded hill in the middle distance, the tall Corinthian columns, the trailing line of cattle with the herdsman hurrying the laggards, all beautifully related. The *Dance by the Waterside* is indeed a lyrical etching with a beautiful distance; a kindred

JACQUES CALLOT: *Beggar*. Etching (M. 703); size
of original, $5\frac{1}{2}'' \times 3\frac{1}{2}''$.

From a print in the British Museum.   53

CLAUDE GELLÉE: *Le Bouvier*. Etching, 3rd state (D. 8); size of original, $5\frac{1}{8}'' \times 7\frac{3}{4}''$.

From a print in the British Museum.

plate even greater in its lovable grace is the *Dance Under the Trees*. Then there is the *Sunset*, full of glowing light, wonderfully rendered and perfectly complete, the vessels in the distance and the figures in the foreground busy with their unloading.

The direct imitation of line engraving seems to have been the aim of Bosse's etching, and much burin work is mixed with his bitten line. The sets of **Abraham Bosse, 1602–1676** *The Seasons* and *Elements* show his hard clear line and precise drawing, and the series of prints depicting the etching and printing workshops of his time are also interesting and provide invaluable records of the methods of the early craftsmen.

The Master of all Etching

The greatest master of all etching, Rembrandt, supreme after three hundred years, for though the modern masters have widened the scope of expres- **Rembrandt, van Ryn, 1606–1669** sion and explored more fully fields of work that he could only open to them, yet he remains unsurpassed and unrivalled in his power, range of vision, and technical skill. The whole of the best of modern etching reflects, in some shape or other, the influence of Rembrandt. Though the tradition of his manner and outlook was submerged during the eighteenth century beneath the popularity of line engraving, yet it was never wholly lost. Andrew Geddes and David Wilkie in the early nineteenth century, modelling their work upon his style, produced prints that were entirely antagonistic to the skilful mechanical reproductive en-graving of the time. Their prints, few though they be, are rightly esteemed to-day, while many a lumber attic holds the work they failed to supplant. In Rembrandt's work can be read an intense introspection, as frank as any autobiography ever penned. The revelation of himself is poignant or gay as the varying fortune of his

life compelled. The comparison of his work and Whistler's
is not only unnecessary, but inimical to the modern
master. Whistler may, in some respects, be the more
accomplished etcher, but he could never depict the
gamut of human experience as Rembrandt so triumphantly
did. From Rembrandt's first known print, the lovely
Portrait of his Mother, to the last, *The Woman with the
Arrow*, there flows a tremendous outpouring of every
shade of human emotion; every phase of experience is
delineated from the purity of the child to the frankly
gross.

From his first etching, the *Portrait of his Mother*,
1628 (H. 1),* remarkable for its freedom of line as much
as for its sure grasp of character, Rembrandt began to
gather a constant increase in command of the bitten
line. We see it in the numerous studies from himself;
in the many etchings of beggars of all types, of which
The Beggar Man and the Woman behind a Bank (H. 13) is
a fine example; in the early scriptural subjects, notably
The Circumcision (H. 19), a gem of beautiful delicate
biting; in the series of studies of old men, of which the
head at the top of the plate of *Three Studies* (H. 25) is
brilliantly direct; and in that extraordinary feat of
craftsmanship, *Diana at the Bath* (H. 42)—through
all these is a progress strongly marked, culminating in
the *Rembrandt's Mother* (H. 52), 1631, a print that has
remained one of the most universally admired of all his
etchings.

The elaborately etched *Rembrandt wearing a Soft
Hat* (H. 54), *The Rat Killer* (H. 97), *Rembrandt with
Plumed Hat* (H. 110), *The Great Jewish Bride* (H. 127),
are four plates rich in colour and fine technical achievement that were produced in the following four years.
The studies of his beloved *Saskia* (H. 145), the *Abraham
casting out Hagar and Ishmael* (H. 149), the *Young Man in*

---

* The reference in brackets is to the number of the print in Professor
A. M. Hind's *Rembrandt's Etchings*.

a Velvet Cap (H. 151—page 59), follow. The last-named is one of the finest of the master's pure etchings. The simplicity of its execution is as remarkable as the characterisation is profound. The placing and the marvellous technique single the plate out among the best of all etched portraiture.

In the great plate *The Death of the Virgin* (H. 161—see page 60), Rembrandt's genius soars to a height of inspired power sublime in its sympathy with the inevitable tragedy of suffering and death that he was later to know so intimately in the early loss of his wife, Saskia.

Malcolm C. Salaman, in a beautifully expressed tribute to the genius of Rembrandt, writes of this print : " The piety, the solemnity, and withal the beauty of death are here, and the scene is realised with wonderful touches of natural truth. Physical finality is graphically suggested in the sinking figure of the Virgin, the powerless, propped-up head, the wasted, pulseless hands; yet, while the sorrowing people around, waiting for the inevitable end, just watch as the bed seems changing to a tomb, there is in the grave atmosphere of the chamber a mysterious uplifting sense of supernatural loveliness, such as one feels with the first far-off, lofty-sounding notes of Croft's music at a Westminster Abbey funeral, and it carries one's eye naturally to the angelic vision— but a few magic strokes of the master's needle."

The splendid portrait of *Rembrandt leaning on a Stone Sill* (H. 168) is of the same year, and its perfect accomplishment is the fruit of the eleven years' ceaseless study that preceded it. His constant search for more expressive utterance led him at times to add to or deface plates that were perfect in themselves. The *Three Heads of Women, one lightly etched* (H. 153), is much finer in its first state with the single head so full of brooding, haunting intensity that it seems to have a kinship to the *Demeter* of Cnidos. How thankful one is that the

charming old woman and baby on the print *Studies
from the Nude* (H. 222) remain, for this little sketch has
a human interest that appeals as strongly as that lovely
drawing of Millet's, *The First Steps.*

With the year 1640 began the landscape etchings,
and, simple in motive as they often are, they have a
weight of truth that has carried an imperishable influence
down through all the best landscape etching since his
death. "The best of Claude or Ruysdael," says Professor A. M. Hind, "is mannered and trivial beside the
sound draughtsmanship and convincing reality of Rembrandt's rendering of nature." The *View of Amsterdam*
(page 63) is a fine example of Rembrandt's landscape
etching. Its quiet literal truth has been a source of
inspiration for much modern landscape etching. It is
very simply and directly treated, and ranks high among
the twenty-seven landscape etchings by Rembrandt, for
it expresses all that is typical of the simple homely
Dutch country. The *Landscape with a Cottage and Hay-
barn* (H. 177), which is perhaps one of the finest he
etched, being exquisite in its arrangement of light and
balance of composition; *The Windmill* (H. 179), with
its wonderful rendering of distance behind the old mill
and its adjacent picturesque house—these are masterpieces. The closely-worked *Cottage with a White Paling*
(H. 203) follows, and how luminous it is! Then comes
the great *Three Trees* (H. 205), the best known and most
completely worked in tone of all Rembrandt's landscape
etchings. The *Omval* (H. 210), of about the same period,
1645, has a beauty and charm that distinguish it even
among the best of the Master's landscapes. The
beautiful quality of line and the certainty of the biting
make the plate one deserving of the closest study. The
contrast between the intricate foreground with the
luminous shadows in which the lovers sit, and the simply
drawn distance that recedes in perfect perspective, is
wonderfully expressed. *Cottage and Farm-buildings with*

REMBRANDT: *Young Man in a Velvet Cap*. Etching (H. 151);
size of original, 3¾″ × 3¼″.

59

REMBRANDT : *The Death of the Virgin*. Etching and Drypoint (H. 161) ; size of original, 16¼″ × 12½″.

From a print in the Victoria & Albert Museum.

a Man Sketching (H. 213) closes the first group of the landscape etchings.

During these five years appeared the two vigorous *Lion Hunt* plates (H. 180 and 181) and *The Raising of Lazarus* (H. 198—see page 64). I have chosen to reproduce this etching because of its extraordinary economy of line. There are only two states of the etching, and the variation is trifling. Compressed within this small plate is an expression of wonder and fear in the presence of the miracle that is without parallel in etching. Of the same period are the *Descent from the Cross—A Sketch* (H. 199) and the *Christ carried to the Tomb* (H. 215). The last is etched with an amazingly free and open line, yet is entirely complete. It reflects Rembrandt's deep understanding of the immeasurable tragedy.

The *Rembrandt drawing at a Window* (H. 229), 1648, is surely one of the most faithful self-portraits ever achieved. It bears the imprint of an absolute searching for self-expression, and is worked in a web of closely-bitten line with additions of drypoint to enrich the tone. So, too, is the famous *Portrait of Jan Six* (H. 228). The amazing masterpiece, *Christ healing the Sick* (H. 236), called "The Hundred Guilder Print"* contains an almost overwhelming amount of interest, diversity of type and action in the swarm of sufferers and their attendants. Every one of the crowded figures is fully and completely expressed, and one can but linger over the immortal print and marvel at the stupendous genius that could wield such power so unaffectedly. All the long study of Rembrandt seems to be infused into this, the most elaborately worked etching he produced, and with its glorious accomplishment of balanced composition and technical skill is united the keen grasp of character

---

* So called because Rembrandt is reputed to have sold the print for 100 guilders—a high price in those days. The highest listed price of this print is £2,700, paid at the Hubert sale in Paris, May 1909.

and deep sympathy he had gathered for suffering and broken humanity.

The second group of landscapes began about 1650, and they were mostly worked with etching and dry-point mixed. They differ in some instances from the earlier landscapes by the introduction of mountainous distances which are not quite convincingly drawn, the *Canal with the Angler* (H. 238) being an example. The *Landscape with Trees, Farm Buildings, and a Tower* (H. 244) is the summit of Rembrandt's achievement in landscape. The brilliant sunlight on the foreground and the trees is emphasised by the dark group of trees in shadow and the threatening storm cloud dragging its length across the sky. *The Gold-weigher's Field* (H. 249) is another great print, and conveys a perfect suggestion of space and distance with the long lines of the foreground sweeping round through the village and the belt of trees to the distance. The great expanse of flat country is expressed with unfaltering selection.

Clement de Jonghe (H. 251) is a portrait of the shrewd print-seller whose activity among the Dutch etchers was widespread. It is beyond doubt one of the finest portraits Rembrandt executed, and the acute personality of the dealer peering out of the picture is wonderfully revealed. It is etched in an open style much simpler than the *Portrait of himself, drawing*. Professor A. M. Hind compares this print with the etchings of Van Dyck, and comments : "With his realisation of the complexity of human nature and in the astounding subtlety of his expression of character in his later portraits he shows a spiritual penetration that Van Dyck never possessed." Rembrandt followed this great print with the *Night Pieces*, of which *The Flight into Egypt* (H. 253) is a brilliant rendering of artificial lighting. It reminds one of the drawing of *The Good Samaritan* in the British Museum, which is so infinitely finer than the elaborate etching of the same subject (H. 101). *Christ Preaching*

REMBRANDT: *View of Amsterdam.* Etching, 2nd state (H. 176); size of original, $4\frac{7}{16}'' \times 6\frac{1}{16}''$.

From a print in the Victoria & Albert Museum.

REMBRANDT: *The Raising of Lazarus.* Etching (H. 198); size of original, $5\frac{7}{8}'' \times 4\frac{1}{2}''$.

64

From a print in the Victoria & Albert Museum.

(H. 256) is a fine example of the later scriptural subjects, the figure of Christ with His uplifted hands being very dignified and the rapt attention of the listening people intensely suggested.

Christ Crucified between the Two Thieves—the *Three Crosses* * (H. 270—page 67). In this great print Rembrandt reaches a height of emotional intensity which places it in a plane above all the other prints of scriptural subjects he etched. Its stupendous strength is tribute to its passionate conception. Professor Hind suggests that the fourth state is inspired by the last agony of Christ. The idea is entirely in keeping with the character of Rembrandt's work, his unwearying effort striving to attain to the highest expression of his subject.

Christ Presented to the People * (H. 271). This magnificent plate also underwent great changes, and that the last state is the finest conception cannot well be denied, for its greater concentration adds much to the power of the composition. Among the scriptural subjects of the last eight years of Rembrandt's etching, the *Presentation in the Temple* (H. 277) is remarkable for the glitter of light on the rich vestments.

The portrait of *Jan Lutma*, the goldsmith (H. 290), is one of the finest of the later portraits, remarkable for its grasp of character and beautiful arrangement of light on the head and dark dress, from which the sensitively drawn hands of the old craftsman gleam out. Contrary to the consensus of critical opinion, I consider the first state the finer, for the more elaborate second state loses, by the addition of the window and the lowering of the dark tones on the wall and the dress, much of the brilliant light that pervades the earlier state.

In a study of Rembrandt's etching it is pre-eminently necessary to consider the evolution of his technique,

---

* These two plates are drypoints. I have included them in this chapter to complete, as far as possible, this appreciation of Rembrandt's work.

F

which was to set the standard for the long series of
etchers succeeding him even down to the living craftsmen. The earlier work is distinguished by its care,
thoroughness, and purity of line.

With the middle period begins the mixture of bitten
line and drypoint, and tonal effects engaged Rembrandt's
attention. The third and last period shows a great increase
in power, and drypoint is used with tremendous effect.

Dutch School contemporary with Rembrandt

Of the Dutch school of etchers contemporary with
and immediately following Rembrandt, only three, Bol,
Lievens and Van Vliet, were strongly influenced by him.
Ostade, entirely individual, influenced Bega and Dusart,
but the landscape etchers were either, like Ruysdael,
entirely Dutch in outlook, or influenced by Italian
study, as shown by the prints of Jan Both and Nicholas
Berchem. The work of the animal painters, Paul
Potter, Carel du Jardin, Dirk Stoop, and Adrian Van de
Velde, presents an entirely new field of subject in etching,
and the sea-pieces of Zeeman and Backhuysen give a
further width of scope to the practice of the art in Holland.

Bol was a pupil of Rembrandt and followed his style
in an imitative manner. Plates such as *The Sacrifice of
Gideon*, *A Philosopher in Meditation*, and
The Family show how closely Bol, with a fine
technique, absorbed the manner of his master.

**Ferdinand Bol,
1616–1680**

Lievens, fellow-student of Rembrandt, was strongly
influenced by him, as the two plates, the *Raising of
Lazarus* and the *St. Jerome*, a very heavily
bitten plate with very dramatic lighting,
clearly show. The *Portrait of a Girl with
Loose Hair* is sensitively etched but lacks the power of
Rembrandt's *Jewish Bride*. Notable among his other
prints are the dignified portrait of *Heinsius* and the very
elaborately worked *Jacob Gouter*.

**Jan Lievens,
1607–1674**

REMBRANDT: *The Three Crosses*. Drypoint, 4th state (H. 270); size of
original, $15\frac{1}{2}'' \times 18''$.

ANTHONIE WATERLOO: *Two Fishermen Starting in a Boat.* Etching (B. 25);
size of original, $3\frac{5}{8}'' \times 5\frac{3}{4}''$.

From a print in the collection of the author.

De Vlieger etched some plates, principally of sea-
coast scenes, of which *Les Pêcheurs* and
Simon de Vlieger, 1601–1653 *Le Transport du Bled* are good examples,
in which the figures are well studied.

Waterloo's plates are of great interest. His *Tobias
and the Angel* is a very elaborate print full of detail.
Two Fishermen Starting in a Boat (B. 25—
Anthonie Waterloo 1610–1676 page 68) is much more open in style and
is an admirable little print, showing his
treatment of Dutch landscape; *Twilight* is another very
interesting plate.

Influenced by a visit to Italy, Jan Both's work is
distinguished by a keen appreciation of
Jan Both 1610–1652 sunlight. *The Ferry* is a good example of
his manner. *Ponte Molle* is an excellent
etching of an ancient bridge near Rome.

Berchem was also strongly influenced by the
Italian school. He drew animals with great skill, but
his work lacks the sturdy native Dutch
Nicolaes Berchem 1620–1683 qualities. *Three Cows resting* and *Crossing
the Brook* are good examples of his manner,
and *The Bagpipes* and *The Flute-player* are other prints
that show the delicate charm of his etchings.

Etcher of some good plates of wild Norwegian landscapes, the novelty of these subjects being so entirely
Allart van Everdingen, 1621–1675 different to the etchings of the flat Dutch
country by the native artists, Everdingen
achieved great success in Holland. *Les
deux nacelles qui s'approchent, Les deux pins près des
chaumières, Les deux hommes sur la terrasse élevée,* and
La nacelle retirée au bord are good examples.

Ostade interpreted the homely scenes of the Dutch
life with unfailing sympathy and power. He was akin
to Burns in his portrayal of rustic pleasures
Adriaen van Ostade, 1610–1685 and the more intimate interiors with the
variety of human interest that he etched
so well. He commanded a perfect technique and ex-

pressed it with entire success. Malcolm Salaman, an enthusiastic admirer of Ostade's etchings, in a note on the Dutch master in his book *The Great Painter Etchers from Rembrandt to Whistler*, admirably expresses Ostade's qualities : " After the supreme master, the greatest Dutch painter etcher was Adrian Van Ostade, of Haarlem, Franz Hal's pupil, and he was absolutely original. In range of subject, pictorial vision and artistic and technical manner he was entirely himself, and a master. His etched line, rich in the expressive quality of the medium, is positively autographic."

The Child asking for a Doll (B. 16 *—page 71) is a charming example of homely humour; the teasing mother and the eager child, admirably drawn, and the figure of the father leaning on the rail resting with entire contentment, completes a beautiful little group. The *Saying Grace* (B. 34) is a little plate full of simple, pious feeling, and the boy's attitude is wonderfully expressive. His etchings of village fairs are full of animation, as the *Fête under the Vine Arbour* (B. 47) and the *Fête under a Large Tree* (B. 48) show by the keen expression of the rustics enjoying their riotous amusements. The *Anglers* (B. 26) is a fine example of his treatment of landscape, and, while it has none of the grandeur and breadth of Rembrandt's finest plates, it is nevertheless distinctive and entirely true to the character of the Dutch landscape. The figures of the anglers hanging over the bridge are admirable. The *Peasant Paying his Score* (B. 42—page 72) is one of the best of Ostade's etchings, showing well his command of technique. The effect of light is full and strong and the figures are charmingly intimate, especially the group round the fire. The *La Chanteuse* (B. 30) illustrates Ostade's sense of humour, the three revellers being exuberantly drawn.

A pupil of Ostade, Bega etched with a powerful,

---

* Adam Bartsch's *Le Peintre Graveur*.

ADRIAEN VAN OSTADE : *The Doll*.   Etching, 3rd state (B. 16);
size of original, $4\frac{1}{8}'' \times 3\frac{1}{8}''$.

ADRIAEN VAN OSTADE: *Peasant Paying his Score.* Etching, 3rd
state (B. 42); size of original, $4\frac{1}{8}'' \times 3\frac{1}{2}''$.

From a print in the British Museum.

vital line, and all his work is boldly drawn. Though he
did not cover so wide a field as Ostade,
Cornelius Bega, 1620–1664 yet in his more limited way he achieved
fine results. *La Mère et son Mari* (B. 35—
page 75) is a characteristic plate, well designed, with
strong contrasts of light and shadow and magnificently
drawn. His *Scène de Taverne, Les Trois Buveurs* (B. 29),
La Jeune Aubergiste (B. 33), and *La Jeune Cabaretière*
(B. 34), should also be seen to appreciate his work.

A follower of Ostade, Dusart used mezzotint and
produced some prints which show very strongly the
influence of his master. Of these *La Fête*
Cornelis Dusart, 1660–1704 *du Village* (B. 16) is strongly drawn and
well observed, and conveys the commotion
of a village fair in convincing fashion, the group of
acrobats at the right of the plate being admirably drawn.
La Ventouse (B. 12) and *Le Chirurgien de Village* (B. 13)
are strongly drawn prints of subjects dealing amusingly
with the rough-and-ready medical methods of the time.
Le Cordonnier (B. 14) is a fine interior.

The Italian influence in style is strongly apparent
in de Laar's work. The *Woman Spin-*
Pieter de Laar, 1600–1650 *ning* (B. 5) and *Hunter with Hounds* (B. 6)
are good examples.

The landscapes of Roghman are interesting for their
study of the treatment of light and shadow. The *View
near Haarlem* (B. 10) is remarkable for its
Roeland Roghman, 1597–1686 lighting, and a plate which well exemplifies
his style is the *Ryswick* (B. 8). *In the
Forest of Seunig* (B. 14) is an etching of trees very complicated in treatment, and the *Landscape with High Rocks
and River*, a plate much simpler in style.

Jardin produced some splendid etchings drawn with
a firm, clear line, and his treatment of
Carel du Jardin, 1622–1678 cattle is, in some ways, finer than any of
the Dutch etchers. The *Two Horses* (B. 4)
is an admirable plate, the foreshortened drawing of the

horse stretched out on the ground being wonderfully true. The *Group of Cattle* (B. 34) with the beast silhouetted against the sky to the left of the plate, is a print that should be studied; while *Dogs* (B. 5), with the sleeping animals basking in the sun, is another good plate. The print *The Two Pigs* (B. 15—page 76) well represents Jardin; the drawing of the animals is superb. But the best known of Jardin's etchings is the *Horseman on the Battlefield* (B. 28), etched with vivid power; the drawing of the corpse of the man in the foreground is especially fine.

Free from the Italian manner, Zeeman's etchings **Reynier Nooms** of Amsterdam and Paris strongly influenced **(Zeeman),** Meryon, the former's *Porte St. Bernard* call-**1623-1663** ing to mind at once the work of the French master. Apart from the interest that Zeeman's etchings of Paris must always arouse to the student from the fact that they were the inspiration of the great French master, the sea-pieces which he etched so convincingly are distinguished for their spirited action, as the series of *Sea Fights* with the picturesque warships of his time show. He etched splendidly the simple Dutch fishing craft, which are but little changed in type to-day. One of the set, *Amsterdam Ships* (B. 68), is reproduced (page 77).

Naiwynx was a follower of Ruysdael, and his etchings have great qualities. The *Landscape with a lofty* **Herman Naiwynx,** *Rock* (B. 2) is a delightful plate with a **1624-1654** beautiful effect of sunny light on the side of the great rock, and the clouds are charmingly drawn. He etched trees with much of the greater master's success.

A famous cattle painter, Potter etched with great effect; the *Horse of Friesland*, with the dark **Paul Potter,** sky throwing the grey horse into sharp **1625-1654** relief, is one of the best known of his prints; and *The Neighing Horse* is another characteristic

CORNELIUS BEGA : *La Mère et son Mari.*   Etching, (B. 30) ;
size of original, $5\frac{1}{4}'' \times 4\frac{3}{8}''$.

75

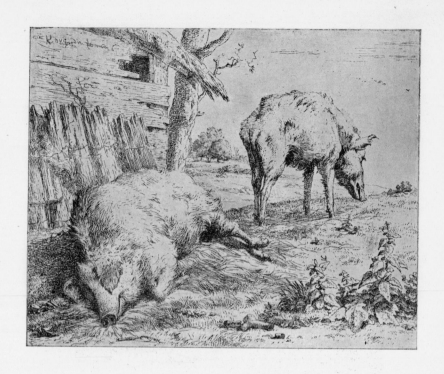

CAREL DU JARDIN: *The Two Pigs.* Etching (B. 15); size of original, $4\frac{3}{4}'' \times 5\frac{7}{8}''$.

From a print in the collection of the author

ZEEMAN : One of the set of *Different Ships of Amsterdam*. Etching (B. 68) ;
size of original, $5\frac{1}{8}'' \times 9\frac{5}{8}''$.

From a print in the possession of the Cotswold Gallery.   77

JACOB RUYSDAEL : *The Three Oaks.*   Etching, 2nd state (B. 6) ; size of original, 5⅛″ × 6″.

From a print in the British Museum.

example of his treatment of cattle subjects; the drawing of the horse is fine and the long, low horizon well
suggests the character of the flat Dutch landscape.
The Bull and *Two Cows* are other notable plates by
Potter.

The great painter, Ruysdael, was one of the best
etchers of the 17th century, and his influence was after-

**Jacob Ruysdael,
1628–1682**

wards deeply felt by the English school,
especially by Crome.   *The Three Oaks* (B. 6
—page 78) is a very notable etching, the
drawing of the trees admirably expressed with a truth
that pervades all his best etchings.   *The Cornfield* (B. 5)
is a little plate with a quiet effect of sunlight.   The more
complicated plates, *The Travellers* (B. 4), with the great
trees in the swamp wonderfully drawn, and *The Little
Bridge* (B. 1), a subject very similar to some of Constable's work (for the English master had a fervent
admiration for Ruysdael), are other fine prints by this
great but unfortunate master.   The etchings of Ruysdael
were quite unappreciated, and he was entirely unsuccess-
ful in interesting the collectors of his time.   His tragic
life ended in abject poverty.

Ludolf Backhuysen, a fine painter of seascapes, only
began etching in the last years of his long life.   He

**Ludolf
Backhuysen,
1631–1708**

studied his subjects with splendid enthusiasm, and etched some plates distinguished
by their truthful rendering and atmospheric
feeling.   The *Distant View of Amsterdam* (B. 5—page
81), *Seascape: Windy Day* (B. 6), and *View of a
Harbour* (B. 9) are good examples.

De Velde etched some well-related landscapes and
cattle subjects.   In the plate *Herdsman and Cattle*

**Adrian van de
Velde,
1635–1672**

Resting the animals are finely drawn, and
the woman and dog below the bare tree
that crosses the corner of the plate, and
the huddled figure of the sleeping man, complete a fine
subject.   *Ox and Sheep* (page 82) is another good

print; the foreshortened drawing of the ox cropping the pasture is excellent.

Seventeenth-century Etching in England

With the advent of Hollar in the household of the Earl of Arundel in 1637, began the history of the British School of Etching. This astounding crafts-

Wenzel Hollar, 1607–1677

man is reputed to have executed 2,700 plates covering an extraordinarily wide and varied field. All subjects came alike to him; he attacked them with zest and achieved remarkable results, even though his work is devoid of the finest qualities of the greatest etchers. In his tribute to Hollar, Malcolm Salaman finely states: "A Thames etching by Hollar, is to one by Whistler, as, say, Macaulay's description of London, in the famous third chapter of the History, compared with Wordsworth's sonnet on Westminster Bridge. Picturesque fact is the motive of one, as suggestive beauty is of the other." Despite the lack of imagination there is an honesty and engaging truth in all his etchings. Whether he was depicting the topographical landscapes—the delightful figure subjects of which the *Winter* (page 83) from the set called *The Small Seasons* is a most intriguing example—or the miraculously etched sets of still-life subjects, such as the *Muffs* and *Shells* (a good example of the latter is reproduced on page 84), the certainty of his needling and biting is amazing. The magnificent etching of *Antwerp Cathedral* and the *Views of London*, so interesting to-day to students of the City's history before the Great Fire, illustrate the value of his work. Wedmore, writing of the fine print, *London from the top of Arundel House*, says: "It has everything that art can give to record of bare fact—except emotion." Drawn from a high elevation it depicts with exquisite gradation the reach of the river to old London Bridge; old St. Paul's, and the

LUDOLF BACKHUYSEN : *Distant View of Amsterdam.*   Etching (B. 4) ; size
of original, 7″ × 9⅜″.

From a print in the British Museum.   81

G

ADRIAEN VAN DE VELDE: *Ox and Sheep*.   Etching (B. 12); size of
original, 5⅜″ × 6⅝″.

From a print in the collection of the author.

WENZEL HOLLAR: *Winter*, from the set of *Small Seasons*.
Etching (P. 617); size of original, 7″ × 5″.

From a print in the British Museum.

WENZEL HOLLAR : *Shells*, from the set of Shells.   Etching (P. 2224);   size
of original, $3\frac{7}{8}'' \times 5\frac{7}{8}''$.

From a print in the British Museum.

numerous towers of the city churches, loom up above the crowded buildings, and the whole scene is beautifully lit, from the dark buildings in the foreground to the faintly bitten lines of the hills in the distance. The sky, though mechanically drawn, is very luminous. *Arundel House* is an etching most certain in its biting and very interesting in its delineation of domestic architecture of the period. *Albury* and the *View from Greenwich* are other prints that should be studied.

Eighteenth-century Etching in Italy, France and Spain

The interest in the remarkable etchings of Tiepolo has of late years become keener, and this master of **Giovanni Battista** the eighteenth-century Italian school should **Tiepolo,** have an assured position in the esteem of **1696–1770** students and collectors. His etchings are distinguished by their brilliance obtained with a very pure technique and their perfectly balanced design. They are often very delicately bitten with an extremely sensitive line. His subjects are of a strange fantastic nature. Magicians, satyrs, and fauns figure frequently, this imagery being sustained at a very high level through all his etched work. The three plates *Punchinello talking to Two Magicians* (page 87), the *Magician and five other figures standing, watching a Serpent* (page 88), and the *Satyr Family, with the Fir Tree* (page 89), are fine examples. Goya and Fragonard were influenced by Tiepolo's etchings; Goya by their bizarre strength and Fragonard by the more delicate idyllic influence.

Canaletto etched with a simple technique entirely individual. His plates express the clear Venetian atmo- **Giovanni Antonio** sphere and sunlight perfectly. In *The* **Canale** *Tower, Malghera*, the suggestive quality of **(Canaletto),** **1697–1768** the line is superb. It is one of the best known and universally admired of all his etchings, and

shows Canaletto's work at its best. The brilliant light on
the white tower and the perfect gradation of tone is con-
veyed by the simplest means. The *Lock at Dolo* with its
charmingly placed figures, of which the little group in the
centre is especially fine, has a beautiful effect of diffused
sunlight and luminous shadow; the arrangement of the
lighting is masterly and a warm glow of colour suffuses
the scene. *Mestre* is a print in which the perspective of
the canal is expressed with the greatest skill. The *Porch
with the Lantern* (page 90) is one of Canaletto's best prints;
the effect of light is simply but surely obtained.

Many of the huge plates of Piranesi consist of
architectural subjects of ancient buildings. *The Temple
of the Sibyl at Tivoli, The Coliseum Rome,*
Giovanni Piranesi, and *Ponte Molle* are characteristic examples.
1720–1778
The series called Carceri are the best of
Piranesi's etchings, for in these plates he depended entirely
on pure etching and discarded the mechanical ruler. They
are most elaborately built up and are replete with harrow-
ing incidentals of torture chambers and dungeons, but
they have little of the terrible impulse of Goya's etchings.

The famous painter, Jean Honoré Fragonard, etched
Fragonard, plates called *The Bacchanales* with a delight-
1732–1806 ful lyrical charm and fantastic daintiness.

Goya is one of the most romantic figures in the
history of art; his work as an etcher is marked by a
strong individuality, expressing a mordant
Francisco Goya, satire on the political and social condition
1746–1828 of Spain in his time. Hamerton in *Etchers
and Etchings* concludes his chapter on the Spanish master
with these words: " His etchings have little artistic
value, and owe their great fame to the fascination of
their incomparable horror and a kind of philosophical
reflection whose bitterness suits our taste." Yet these
etchings have great dramatic power, and among them
are many examples of magnificent draughtsmanship of a
direct strength that is amazing. *A Caza de dientes*, No. 12

G. B. TIEPOLO: *Punchinello talking to Two Magicians.* Etching
(de V. 21); size of original, $9\frac{1}{4}'' \times 7\frac{1}{4}''$.

From a print in the British Museum.

87

G. B. TIEPOLO: *Magician and five other figures standing,*
watching a Serpent. Etching (de V. 24); size of original, $8\frac{7}{8}'' \times 6\frac{7}{8}''$.

88 From a print in the British Museum.

G. B. TIEPOLO: *Satyr Family, with the Fir Tree.* Etching (de
V. 22); size of original, $8\frac{7}{8}'' \times 7''$.

CANALETTO: *The Porch with the Lantern.* Etching, 1st state (de V. 10); size of
original, $11\frac{7}{8}''$ × $17''$.

From a print in the possession of the Cotswold Gallery.

of *Los Caprichos* (page 93), is a print which is pregnant with the morbid passion of Goya's work. The drawing of the hanged man is extraordinarily powerful and the line is less coarse than in many of the plates. The simple tone of aquatint in the sky is of great help to the design. *Se aprovechan* and *Enterrar y callar* are two plates in the series called *The Disasters of War* that are terrible in their sheer horror. The drawing of the stripped bodies and their despoilers is masterly. The series *The Bull Fighters* convincingly conveys the varying phases of the national spectacle of Spain, its daring and its tragedy. *La Même Ceballos monté sur un taureau*, a very vigorous plate, and *Mort Malheureuse de Pepe Illo* are good examples. The later editions of Goya's plates give little idea of the brilliance of the early proofs, the aquatint tones are worn away and the line too has suffered badly, and to appreciate the mordant genius of the Spanish master to its full and proper extent the finest early editions must be studied; they are most easily found in the Print Room at either the British Museum or South Kensington Museum.

English Etchers of the Nineteenth and Twentieth Centuries

While Crome and Turner produced bitten plates, the best of the work of Wilkie, Geddes, Daniel and Read was done with the drypoint, and their prints will be dealt with in the following chapter on Drypoints. The principal plates of Cotman were soft ground, and these are also dealt with elsewhere.

The Norwich Master, Crome, was the first great painter of the British School to produce etchings completely expressed with a clean line. *Mousehold Heath* (page 94) is generally held to be the finest of his plates. The sky is one of the best ever etched and the character of the landscape is extra-

John Crome, 1768–1821

ordinarily faithfully drawn. The *Hall Moor Road near Hingham* is another very fine example of Crome's etching, in which the oaks are splendidly drawn; the plate loses a great deal in the last state by the coarsely bitten lines across the sky. The *Composition*, the large *Sandy Road through Woodland, Footbridge at Cringleford, Back of the New Mills, Gravel Pit, Marlingford* and *At Bawburgh* should all be closely studied, for they are unrivalled for keen characterisation of tree growth and magnificent drawing.

The etchings of Turner were bitten as a foundation for the mezzotint engraver to work upon, and though

Joseph Mallord William Turner, 1775–1851
they were for this reason simply drawn and strongly bitten, they are marvellously suggestive with the utmost economy of line.
His superb draughtsmanship and power of design are displayed in the etchings for the three *Liber Studiorum* plates, the *Junction of the Severn and the Wye*, the *Stork and Aqueduct*, and *Winchelsea, Sussex* (page 95).

Of the lesser known etchers of the Norwich school, the work of Stannard deserves much more attention

Joseph Stannard, 1797–1830
than it has received. His luminous print, *A Composition* (page 96), is a good example of his excellent use of clear well-bitten line.

The etchings of Palmer have evoked much controversy, and many critics have hotly contested their

Samuel Palmer, 1805–1881
merit as etchings, but their spiritual and romantic power cannot be denied. They have an individuality that impresses them indelibly upon the minds of all who can perceive their great qualities. Elaborate in detail as no other etchings ever were before them, they are yet perfectly knit together in effect.

The serene charm of *The Early Ploughman* (page 99) is the outcome of great poetical feeling and magnificent technique. Hamerton, writing of *The Early Ploughman*,

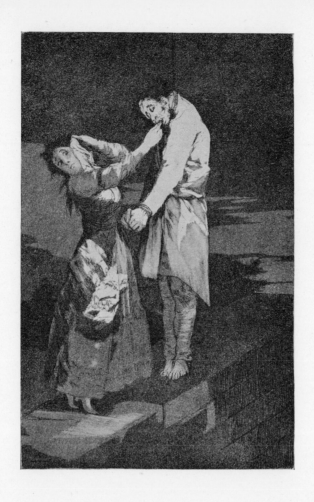

FRANCISCO GOYA: *A Caza de dientes*. Etching and
Aquatint (H. 12); size of original, 8½″ × 6″.

From a print in the Victoria & Albert Museum.

JOHN CROME : *Mousehold Heath*. Etching (T. 3); size of original, 8⅛″ × 11″.

From a print in the collection of Mr. Harold J. L. Wright.

JOSEPH MALLORD WILLIAM TURNER: *Winchelsea*. Etching (R. 42); size of original, $8\frac{1}{8}'' \times 11\frac{1}{4}''$.

JOSEPH STANNARD: *A Composition.* Etching; size of original, $5\frac{7}{8}'' \times 8\frac{1}{4}''$.

From a print in the collection of Mr. Martin Hardie, R.E.

in his eloquent tribute to Palmer, says : " Many a night
has the etcher of this plate wandered in a land of beauty
from sunset to sunrise, from twilight to twilight, from
the splendour of the west to the splendour of the east,
watching through the gradual changes of the hours,
and gathering for us that rare learning of which his works
are full." The extraordinary depth of luminous shadow,
the light which suffuses the whole scene, and the perfect
relation of the beautiful sky to the misty distance are
all achieved with consummate skill. Intricate as his
style was, Palmer depended entirely upon his line, which
was never obscured with ink in the printing, but always
stands clearly revealed. The whole of Palmer's etchings,
thirteen in all, are worthy of the closest examination.
Among them *The Herdsman* (page 100) is a magnificent
treatment of moonrise. The moon rising over the dark
hills is indeed Shelley's " bright orbéd maiden with white
fire laden," for its light gleams through all the lovely
landscape, over the dark valley on to the trees and the
oxen with the herdsman in the foreground. *The Rising
Moon* is another poetical print of a similar character,
while *The Morning of Life* shows how finely Palmer could
envisage the glowing glamour of sunlight. Martin
Hardie has finely stated the chief glory of Palmer's
etchings : " No one has rendered more impressively
than he the sentiment of spiritual and ideal beauty
immanent in landscape."

The work of the famous etcher Seymour Haden, the
surgeon, is one of the most remarkable features in the
Sir Francis history of etching. That a man busy
Seymour Haden, and successful in an exacting profession
1818–1910 should turn to an equally exacting art
and achieve such masterpieces with consummate ease
is simply astounding. Further, not only by his work
did he provide a new stimulating influence on etching,
but by his writing he impressed his theories and outlook
firmly and indelibly on the mind of succeeding generations.

H

He etched with a quick, simple suggestion and free,
vigorous line that sometimes leave his prints almost
incomplete. His was the successful faculty of selection,
possible only to a mind acute and alert in instant trans-
mission of impulse, which he recorded rapidly and
unhesitatingly.

Many of his plates were etched out of doors, and are to
all intents and purposes beautiful drawings, some of them
showing a completeness of design that is wonderful. The
Kilgaren Castle (page 101) is a very fine example of this.
The *Water Meadow* is a beautiful plate with a tenderly
etched sky most perfectly suggesting the summer shower.
In the large plate the *Breaking up of the Agamemnon*,
the sky is extraordinarily fine with a most beautiful
suggestion of colour and light. *Erith Marshes* is an etching of great breadth and power.

The etchings of the *Punch* artist, Keene, display
his wonderful draughtsmanship to great advantage.
The Lady with a Book and *The French Peasant* are examples of his command
of the bitten line.

Charles Keene, 1823–1891

Whistler began the long series of his etchings
with the famous sketches on the Government coastal
survey plates, which were the cause of
Whistler's retiring from the United States
service. In France he worked among the
masters who were active in reviving the general practice
of etching after its long neglect. He was well equipped
to rival any of his fellow-artists, and the first French
set shows that he was already a master-etcher, sure of
his utterance with the line and with a keen appreciation
of the possibilities of the medium—possibilities he was
later to explore and exemplify with such wonderful
results.

James McNeill Whistler, 1834–1903

The French plates reveal a close observation and
were etched with elaborate detail, and in all of them there
is a sincere search for personal expression. *La Vieille*

SAMUEL PALMER: *The Early Ploughman.* Etching, touched proof (H. 9) ; size
of original, 5¼″ × 7¾″.

From a print in the collection of Mr. Martin Hardie, R.E.   99

SAMUEL PALMER: *The Herdsman*. Etching, early state (H. 8); size of original,
$5\frac{1}{4}'' \times 7\frac{3}{4}''$.

From a print in the collection of Mr. Martin Hardie, R.E.

SIR F. SEYMOUR HADEN : *Kilgaren Castle*. Etching (H. 65) ; size of original,
$4\frac{3}{8}'' \times 5\frac{7}{8}''$.

From a print in the collection of Mr. Martin Hardie, R.E.

J. A. McN. WHISTLER: *The Unsafe Tenement.* Etching, 4th state (K. 17); size
of original, 6⅛″ × 8¾″.

From a print in the collection of Mr. Harold J. L. Wright.

aux Loques : how wonderfully drawn is the old woman sitting among the medley of her chattels; the sensitive delicacy of the head and hands is superb and the arrangement of the plate is perfect. *The Unsafe Tenement* (page 102) displays Whistler's skill with the needle in the wonderful drawing and variety of texture suggested and the treatment of light and shadow. It is peculiarly a plate for the student to study, for Whistler's advance from this downright plate to the magical suggestion of his Venice sets was along the path of hard work and rigid training, and in no way the result of caprice.

The Thames set brought forth fresh qualities, for with these etchings—by some still held to be his finest work—he developed a technique as marvellous as Rembrandt's. These Thames-side subjects are wrought with an intricate variety of line and contrast of light and shade, and some of them are bitten with miraculous certainty. *The Limeburner, Eagle Wharf, Black Lion Wharf, Longshoremen, Rotherhithe* are masterpieces in their keen observation and accuracy. Hollar's manner is rightly coupled with them in speaking of their topographical truth, but how they transcend the early master's work in their exquisite poetry; among the portraits of Whistler's early period the *Becquet* is a splendid example.

The Venice sets reveal the master definitely developing from the manner of his previous etchings and forming a style peculiarly his own. They are unapproachable in the elimination of all but the very essentials needed to form the beautiful pattern of line and tone.

The Palaces (second state), with the beautiful façades of the stately old buildings, poetically conceived and drawn with consummate skill, and the graceful gondolas woven into a lovely pattern as they are strung along the edge of the canal. *The Doorway :* the arrangement of this plate is most beautiful and the interior is enchantingly luminous. *The Beggars :* Whistler here takes as his subject a covered alley-way, and by magical skill

in contrasting sunlight and shadow creates a print of
exquisite beauty. The *Two Doorways:* this exquisite
rendering of the doorways on the bend of the canal is
extraordinarily fine. The print shows all the best
qualities of Whistler's manner. Note the perfect design,
the luminous shadows, the admirable suggestion of texture
and the subtle drawing of the receding houses by the
canal. *The Traghetto* (No. 2) : this famous plate is generally considered one of Whistler's masterpieces. The
placing and drawing of all the various figures and the
glamour of the lighting are alike incomparable.

The Second Venice Set: the *Quiet Canal*, with the
tall houses overhanging the limpid water ; the haunting,
mysterious *Furnace Nocturne ;* the delicately bitten
Bead Stringers, and *The Balcony* (page 105) are fine
examples. In the later plates Whistler somewhat
returned to his earlier manner, but there is a greater
amount of detail and a fuller tone, though all the grace
and beauty of the Venetian plates is retained.

The Balcony, Amsterdam (page 106), shows to the full
his later manner, being marvellously rich in tone and
colour, and perfect in design. With *The Embroidered
Curtain, The Steps,* and the *Long House Dyers, Amsterdam,*
of the Amsterdam set, Whistler reached the summit
of his achievement as etcher.

Tireless in his search for perfection, he altered plates
time and again, and ruthlessly destroyed them if they
failed to satisfy his exacting demands. In the sustained
quality of his etchings Whistler is unsurpassed ; in beauty
of arrangement, treatment of the witchery of light,
and suggestion of colour, he is incomparable. His
influence has been potent ; in no way has it benefited
the imitative followers who could gather nothing from
their adoration of his prints but a facility for creating
pretty patterns and feeble echoes of his manner ; on
the other hand, the discerning student may be inspired
by an appreciation of the master's great endeavour and

J. A. McN. WHISTLER : *The Balcony, Venice.* Etching
(K. 207); size of original, $11\frac{5}{8}'' \times 7\frac{7}{8}''$.

From a print in the British Museum.

J. A. McN. WHISTLER: *The Balcony, Amsterdam.*
Etching (K. 405) ; size of original, $10\frac{5}{8}'' \times 6\frac{7}{8}''$.

From a print in the Victoria & Albert Museum.

ALPHONSE LEGROS : *The Dying Vagabond*. Etching
and sand-ground Aquatint (M.-T. 89); size of original,
21⅝″ × 15⅜″.

From a print in the Victoria & Albert Museum.

SIR J. C. ROBINSON: *Corfe Castle: Sunshine after Rain.* Etching (H. 16);
size of original, $6\frac{1}{4}'' \times 11''$.

　　　　　　　　　　　From a print in the possession of Messrs. Colnaghi.

signal success in creating, from the solid foundation of sound craftsmanship, the most beautiful expression in etching since Rembrandt.

A great painter and one of the greatest etchers of the 19th century, Legros' prints bear the mark of a
Alphonse Legros, 1837–1911
profound mind, lofty outlook and austere style. They are utterly divorced from all but the highest ideals, and though they recall the work of many of the old masters, they have a great individuality and dignity that lifts them above all the etchings of the modern school. They are in number over seven hundred.

Legros began etching in Paris at the period when Bracquemond, Haden, and Whistler were publishing their work, and his early prints included some illustrations to Edgar Allan Poe's works, of a grim and weird nature thoroughly in keeping with the tales themselves. Among the finest prints of his early period are *The Communion in the Church of St. Médard, The Spanish Singers*, and *The Procession through the Vaults of St. Médard*, all of which are of a deep imaginative character, dramatic and intensely felt. *The Dying Vagabond* (page 107), a great plate, is a masterpiece that awes by the terrible power with which the pitiable tragedy is portrayed. Wedmore finely said that this plate " is type, or final expression, of Legros' leaning towards the theme of the human derelict." The sombre, tragic print *Death and the Woodman* reflects the deep melancholy of Legros' outlook. His portraits of *Cardinal Manning, G. F. Watts, Victor Hugo*, and *Auguste Rodin* are marked with a deep and expressive dignity that no modern etcher but he could achieve.

The landscape etchings of this master have a wide range of expression, from the tender plates *A Sunny Meadow* and *The Sheep-fold*, to the power of *The Storm*, with its fine rain-swept sky, and *The Abbey Farm*, with its dark trees and buildings against a dramatic sky. *The*

Plain is a wide, open stretch of country beautifully drawn. *The Canal* (*Morning*) is a fine treatment of trees by the riverside, a theme that Legros constantly returned to with very poetic results. The dark gloom of the forest is convincingly recorded in the print *In the Forest of Conteville*.

Legros by his teaching at South Kensington and the Slade School exercised a very great and lasting influence. Among his pupils were William Strang and Sir Charles Holroyd.

In treatment of atmospheric effects, the work of Sir J. C. Robinson holds a unique position among modern **Sir John Charles** etching. That some of the thirty plates **Robinson,** which form the total of his prints are **1824–1913** overworked, should not prevent a keen appreciation of such fine prints as *Corfe Castle : Sunshine after Rain* (page 108), *Swanage Down,* and *Space and Light,* which are entirely successful.

Finely designed and vigorously executed with a clear expressive line, the best of the prints of Holroyd are **Sir Charles** sure of a permanent place in the history **Holroyd,** of modern etching. The beneficent in- **1861–1917** fluence of Legros over Holroyd is strongly apparent in many of his etchings. The *Monte Oliveto* series contains some fine plates, notably the *Ladies' Guest House,* and the *Cypress Trees near Siena ; Langstrath,* the *Nymphs of the Sea,* and the fine *Flight into Egypt* are thoroughly representative works.

Of all the living etchers there is not one more versatile than Sir Frank Short. It would be difficult adequately **Sir Frank Short,** to estimate the influence of this master **R.A., P.R.E.,** craftsman and teacher on the etchers of **1857–** to-day. His work in the school of etching and engraving at the Royal College of Art has been universally recognised in generous measure, and by none more heartily than his pupils. In every branch of etching and engraving he has achieved a complete know-

SIR FRANK SHORT: "*The Street*," *Whitstable*. Etching (S. 290, supplement);
size of original, 13½″ × 9½″.

From a print in the possession of the author.

WILLIAM STRANG: *Rudyard Kipling*, 1898. Etching (S. 345); size of original, 14″ × 10″.

From a print in the collection of Mr. Harold J. L. Wright.

D. Y. CAMERON: *Damme*. Etching and Drypoint (R. 391);
size of original, 10⅛″ × 7⅜″.

From a print in the private collection of Mr. T. Connell.

I

F. BRANGWYN: *Hop-pickers*. Etching (No. 207); size of original, $24\frac{3}{4}'' \times 37\frac{1}{4}''$.

From a print in the possession of the Fine Art Society.

ledge and magnificent mastery, and has given that hard-
won knowledge and experience in munificent generosity
to all who have been wise enough to profit by it.   Always
he has practised a pure, honest technique, and a survey
of his bitten etchings will surely convince the student
that no etcher ever excelled Sir Frank Short in the use
of inspired and expressive line.

His etchings are distinguished by their poetic reticence
—a quality that is all too rare in the clamorous restless-
ness of much of the work of to-day.   *Low Tide and the
Evening Star and Rye's Long Pier Deserted* is the plate
that is usually considered Sir Frank's masterpiece;
it is undoubtedly an etching of the highest rank full of
quiet, poetic power.   " *The Street," Whitstable* (page 111)
is a most original etching and an excellent example
of the purity of the master's line.   It is a fine treatment
of a subject that few etchers would be tempted to portray.
*Windy Day in Kent, Unloading Peat, Dort, Angler's Bridge
on the Wandle* are three other fine plates.

I think it is the deep spiritual understanding derived
from communing with all the aspects of nature that has
made the brooding beauty of many of Sir Frank Short's
prints so profound.   The master told me one day in
Ramsgate that he used to meet the Abbot of the Priory
there on the cliffs and they would together watch the
dawn rise.   Once the abbot turned to him and, with a
wave of his hand to the sleeping town, said : " They
who sleep there do not know what they miss."

Among the great number of Strang's etchings are
many prints of great strength and power, for though
he was influenced by Rembrandt, Holbein,
William Strang Millet and, more strongly, by his master,
1859–1921 Legros, his own personality is nevertheless
powerful, and he produced prints that will live.   The
illustrations to *Pilgrim's Progress* are splendidly attuned
to the famous allegory.   *The Muckrake* and *Christian
and Hopeful in the Dungeon* are fine examples.   *Socialists*

shows Strang's qualities at their fullest, his sardonic
humour and keen appreciation of the character of the
speaker and his motley audience. *The Cause of the Poor*
is a plate of similar character, powerful in drawing and
characterisation. His portraits are among the finest
work in modern etching. *J. B. Clark, Cosmo Monkhouse,
Robert Louis Stevenson, Cunninghame Graham*, and the
magnificent *Kipling* (page 112) are among the best.
His etched illustrations to the Kipling tales are very
notable, and few etchings since Goya have such morbid
power.

David Young Cameron has produced many notable
etchings and not a few masterpieces. The fine plate

David Young
Cameron,
1865– called *The Border Tower* well represents
his early manner, and the *Loches* is a magnificent example of his later manner in
which drypoint is added to the etched work, and a great
power of strong contrasts and rich colour is achieved.
Roberts Lee's Workshop is an interior full of delicate light
and luminous shadow, and the intricate detail with which
it is filled is fused together with great skill. *The Meuse*
is the finest landscape of Cameron's later manner, with
a deep romantic feeling and splendid atmospheric effect.
The wide sweep of the river below the hills crowned with
the citadel and castle is magnificently drawn. *Evening
on the Findhorn* has the same deep spiritual feeling;
the sky with its wonderful suggestion of the sinking sun
is extraordinarily luminous. *Interior, Notre Dame, Dinant*
is a fine architectural plate with the altar blazing with
light in the dark chancel. *The Five Sisters* is Cameron's
masterpiece; the tremendous effect of height and suggestion of the glorious colour of the stained glass place
the print among the finest modern etchings. *The Canon-
gate Tolbooth, Edinburgh* is another fine architectural
subject, while the well-balanced *Dinant*, with the long
quayside and old houses, *Damme* (page 113), the lovely

GEORGE CLAUSEN: *Filling Sacks*. Etching (G. 29); size of original, 11½″ × 9½″.

From a print in the possession of Messrs. Colnaghi.

GEORGE CLAUSEN: *A Journey by Night*. Etching and Mezzotint (G. 19); size
of original, $4\frac{3}{4}'' \times 6\frac{1}{4}''$.

118   From a print in the possession of Messrs. Colnaghi.

AUGUSTUS JOHN: *Benjamin Waugh.*   Etching (D. 23); size of original,
$6\frac{7}{16}'' \times 5\frac{7}{8}''$.

From a print in the collection of Mr. T. F. Clarke.

PERCY FRANCIS GETHIN : *The Terrace, Compiègne.* Etching; size of original,
7⅞″ × 11¾″.

From a print in the collection of Mr. Harold J. L. Wright.

proportioned tower looming up against the dark sky, and the *St. Laumer-Blois* are other fine plates by the Scottish master.

Whatever may be the feelings of the lover of the orthodox etched line when contemplating the huge etchings of Brangwyn, an honest admiration must be given to his tremendous power and range. His subjects cover a very wide field, and the great plates he etches are designed with a massive sense of construction and balance. The series of the *Earthquake Ruins at Messina* are powerful plates, of which *L'Immaculata* is a characteristic example. The early *Assisi*, *Old Hammersmith* and *Road in Picardy* are much more dependent on their line than his late work, in which the clever printing is used to give force to the strongly contrasted light and tone. *Windmill Bruges, Canon Street, Bridge at Albi, Hop-pickers* (page 114) and the great *Breaking up of the Caledonia* are thoroughly representative works.

Frank Brangwyn, 1867–

Though the paintings and water-colours of the great poet-painter, George Clausen, are justly acclaimed, the power of his work as an etcher is not yet fully recognised. *Filling Sacks* (page 117), *Cleaning Wheat*, and *The Barn Door* are etchings of interiors of the old barns that he has painted so finely, and all three are distinguished by sure design, superb character of drawing, and beauty in arrangement of light and shadow. Among his landscape etchings, *Clavering Fields* and *September Morning* are drawn with convincing truth of atmospheric effect; the *September Morning* is especially beautiful. The night effects, *A Journey by Night* (page 118)—an etching strengthened with mezzotint—and the lovely aquatint, *A Starry Night*, are prints deeply poetical in conception and treatment.

George Clausen, 1852–

Technically derived from Rembrandt, as the early

self-portraits clearly show, the etched work of Augustus
John contains some prints of the greatest
Augustus John, interest.   The portraits of *Charles McEvoy,*
1879–
William Rothenstein and *Benjamin Waugh*
(page 119) are especially fine, and other prints that
display his vivid, powerful drawing are the *Maggie : A
Village Child, The Pheasant, Head of a Gypsy, The Jewess,
Lady with a Necklace* and *The Old Haberdasher.*

The few etchings of that fine draughtsman, Gethin, are
esteemed for their beautiful qualities of design and
treatment; his untimely death in France
P. F. Gethin, while serving in the British Army cut short
1874–1916
a career full of promise. *The Coliseum,
Auxerre, Gerona,* and *The Terrace, Compiègne* (page 120)
are all fine etchings.

No living etcher is more various in subject and treatment than James McBey, who, from his first plates
etched in Aberdeen in 1902, has pursued
James McBey, a course of sustained advance in achieve-
1883–
ment that has made his etchings justly
apprised. Among the 200 prints that form the output
of McBey to the latest of his plates, there are undoubted
masterpieces which by their power of suggestion and sure
grasp of essentials take rank among the finest etchings
produced by any modern master. Subjects so utterly
different as the interior *Night in Ely Cathedral* and the
extraordinarily original *Dawn* of the first Palestine set
show how wide is the range of McBey's work. In the
long sequence of fine plates that he has produced may be
singled out the *Sea and Rain, Macduff* (page 123), with
its effect of storm rendered vividly, with a vibrant suggestion of the great seas washing over the harbour break-
water, *The Moray Firth,* a beautifully designed and bitten
plate, the *Penzance,* with its finely etched sky, and *The
Lion Brewery,* a beautiful arrangement, most skilfully
etched, and generally held to be the best of his London
etchings, though *The Pool* is in every way as fine. *The*

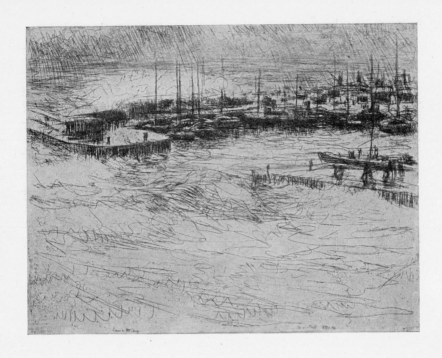

JAMES McBEY: *Sea and Rain, Macduff*. Etching; size of original, 6⅜″ × 8½″.

From a print in the collection of Mr. Martin Hardie.

JAMES McBEY: *The Torpedoed " Sussex."* Etching; size of original, 8⅛″ × 15⅛″.

From a print in the collection of Mr. Martin Hardie, R.E.

ERNEST S. LUMSDEN : *The Scales*. Etching; size of original
14″ × 9¾″.

From a print in the possession of Messrs. P. and D. Colnaghi.

THÉODORE ROUSSEAU: *Chênes de Roche*. Etching (L. D. 4); size of original,
5¼″ × 8¼″.

From a print in the possession of Messrs. Colnaghi.

Torpedoed " Sussex " (page 124) is undoubtedly the best of the French plates; it has all the finest qualities of McBey's art, perfectly balanced design, great atmospheric suggestion, masterly technique and amazingly direct statement.

Few etchers have succeeded as Lumsden has in render-

Ernest S. Lumsden, 1883– ing successfully the spell of India. *Benares No. 2, Jodhpur from the Desert, The Bazaar : Jodhpur, The Umbrella* and the two magnificent interiors, *The Lamas* and *The Scales* (page 125), are among the finest prints he has yet produced.

Among other British etchers, notable work is being done by E. Blampied, G. Brockhurst, F. Burridge, F. L. Griggs, Lee Hankey, Martin Hardie, Malcolm Osborne, H. Rushbury, George Soper, R. Spence, and W. Walcot.

CONTINENTAL ETCHERS OF THE NINETEENTH AND TWENTIETH CENTURIES

The Barbizon painter, Rousseau, was one of the earliest

Theodore Rousseau, 1812–1867 etchers of the revival in France. His prints show strongly the influence of Ruysdael. *Chênes de Roche* (page 126) is a good illustration of his fine draughtsmanship of trees.

Charles Jacque was indefatigable, and among his immense output are many plates of splendid quality.

Charles Jacque, 1813–1894 Influenced by the great Dutch masters, he studied their work very closely, and many copies of Rembrandt, Ostade and Du Jardin show the source of much of the splendid technique he acquired. His influence on modern etching was great and beneficent, for he was one of the pioneers of the revival of etching in the nineteenth century in France, and his work, with its fine, honest, searching technique, should be closely studied. Though he lacked the power and lofty dignity of his friend Millet, yet his work is distinguished with an intimate poetry that compels an ungrudging admiration. Especially beautiful are his plates *Le Bergerie Béarnaise*, an etching of sheep that is a miracle of technique, and *Troupeau de Porcs*, which is generally considered his masterpiece. Among his earlier work his *Tueurs de Cochons* is a little gem. Jacque's etchings deserve far more attention, both from collectors and students, than they have hitherto received. Most of the more famous plates by Jacque contain animals, which he drew with superb skill; he understood them intimately as few artists ever did. *La Bergerie* is an interior as remarkable for its beautiful lighting as for the skilfully drawn sheep. Of his landscape prints the following should be studied: *Troupeau de Porcs sortant d'un Bois*, *Le Repos Paysage*, *Dans le Bois*—a plate of great interest, the bare trees finely drawn. *La Rentree*, with the sheep crowded into the narrow entrance to the barn, the charming *Laveuse*, and *L'Enfant Prodigue* (page 129) are other fine prints.

Jacque had a most extraordinary, varied career. He was in turn clerk, topographical engraver, soldier— he served for five years—and an illustrator; and while at Barbizon he owned a poultry farm and wrote a standard work, illustrated by himself, on the subject of chicken rearing.

The great painter, Millet, with his instinctive power of expressing the finest qualities of the various media he used, was eminently successful as an **Jean Francois Millet, 1814–1875** etcher. The work of Jacque was well known to Millet, and he probably derived a good working knowledge of the technique of etching from his friend. There are, however, several prints which show how Millet experimented with the various methods and tools. Though only thirteen etchings form the total finished work of Millet on the copper, yet he was assuredly a master-etcher. Every one of these etchings is conceived in the true spirit of the art, with a firm, expressive line full of vitality and truth, and though

CHARLES JACQUE: *L'Enfant Prodigue.* Etching (G. 137); size of original, $4\frac{1}{2}'' \times 7\frac{1}{8}''$.

From a print in the collection of Mr. Frank L. Emanuel.

K

J. F. MILLET: *Two Men Digging*.   Etching, 4th state (L. D. 13) ; size of original,
9⅜″ × 13¼″.

From a print in the collection of Mr. Harold J. L. Wright.

J. F. MILLET: *Woman Feeding her Child*.   Etching (D. **17**); size of
original, $7\frac{3}{8}'' \times 6\frac{1}{4}''$.

From a print in the collection of the author.   131

J. B. C. COROT : *Souvenir D'Italie*.   Etching (D. 5) ; size of
original, $11\frac{5}{8}''\times 8\frac{3}{4}''$.

From a print in the British Museum.

his subjects are those he painted, yet there is not a hint of reproduction in one of them. There is a note in Sensier's fine biography of Millet which is interesting to the student : " Meryon, who has had such success since with his etchings, had a great opinion of Millet's, and took the trouble to print some proofs in his own press, in order to study their qualities."

Millet etched subjects of the life and labour of the peasant with a reticent power derived from the know-ledge he had acquired in his youth, while working on his father's farm in the little hamlet of Gruchy near Cher-bourg. It was all in his very bones. He knew inti-mately all the varying tasks that come to the peasants with the changing seasons, the digging, sowing and the harvest, and the simple home-life of the women busy with their manifold household duties or tending the sheep in the fields. The *Two Men Digging* (page 130) is a noble print, the action of the peasants working at the stubborn soil, with the rhythmical swing of their spades, caught and expressed with a conviction of truth that only a man who had shared in their arduous toil could attain. In the *Man with a Wheelbarrow*, his arms rigid with the weight of the load, the poise of the figure is superb; the very sway of the head is suggested, and there is a beautiful glow of light in this, one of the finest of Millet's prints. The little plate, *Man leaning on his Spade*, has the same intimate quality; weariness is woven through the lines on the plate. The three single-figure subjects, the *Woman Sewing*, the *Woman Churning*, and the *Wool-carder*, are drawn with a grave impressive fidelity. Of the three the *Woman Churning* is the finest etching, its line is finely expressive and the lighting of the figure masterly. The *Woman Feeding her Child* (page 131) is a superb etching in its simplicity of execution and sober, unaffected dignity, and the small plate, *The Vigil*, with the intent women working by candlelight, is a poetical treatment of artificial light. There is a beautiful glow of morning light in the largest plate that Millet etched, the *Peasants starting for Work ;* the lovely *Shepherdess Knitting,* too, is full of light, and the *Gleaners,* though it so closely follows in composition the famous painting, is as complete and independent in its linear expression as the famous lithograph, *The Sower,* is independent of the same subject in painting. The *Shepherd Girl Spinning* is the lightest in biting of all Millet's etchings.

A few charmingly expressive plates bear the name of Corot, though he can hardly be ranked among the great etchers, for he only drew his subjects upon the copper, while the biting—the actual etching—was done by his friend Bracquemond. But, as may be seen in the prints, called *Dans les Dunes,* *L'Etang de Ville d'Avary, Environs de Rome,* a very beautiful design, and *Souvenir d'Italie* (page 132), he drew with the selective instinct of the etcher.

Jean Baptiste Camille Corot, 1796–1875

Daubigny etched a large number of plates. The earliest are full of delicate detail and subtle effect, and their technical quality is very high. His later work is broader and freer, and he depicted pastoral themes with poetic suggestion. The influence of Claude is strongly apparent in many of the plates, especially in a beautiful print called *Cows in a Pool. The Satyr* is a very finely etched plate, full of wonderful, glowing light. *The Ford, The Sheepfold, Shepherd and Shepherdess* (page 135), *Morning, Temps d'Orange,* and the winter landscape, *Crows perching in a Tree,* are other fine examples.

Charles Francis Daubigny, 1817–1878

In the history of art there is no tragedy so poignantly complete as the life of Charles Meryon—that inspired, haunted visionary, whose morbid, brooding soul is tremendously revealed in the etchings known as the Paris set. He is among the few supreme etchers, a master unapproached in his own field, his technique and treatment being firm, searching, and eminently fitted to his subjects. Born

Charles Meryon, 1821–1868

CHARLES F. DAUBIGNY: *Shepherd and Shepherdess*. Etching
(D. 122); size of original, 10″ × 7¾″.

Insatiable vampire l'éternelle Luxure
Sur la Grande Cité convoite sa pâture.

CHARLES MERYON: *Le Stryge*. Etching, 1st state
(L. D. 23); size of original, $6\frac{3}{4}'' \times 5\frac{1}{8}''$.

From a print in the collection of Mr. T. Simpson.

CHARLES MERYON: *Le Petit Pont*. Etching, 3rd state
(L. D. 24); size of original, $9\frac{7}{8}''\times7\frac{1}{4}''$.

From a print in the collection of Mr. Hugh Stokes.

137

CHARLES MERYON: *La Morgue*. Etching (L.D. 36); size of original, 9″ × 8¼″.

From a print in the British Museum.

under the cloud of illegitimacy which darkened his outlook all his life, and caused him to relinquish his service in the French Navy after cruises to the South Seas and the Mediterranean, Meryon, during these voyages, made sketches which he afterwards used for etchings, but with no great results. After leaving the Navy he began to study painting, but, finding that he was afflicted with colour-blindness, he turned to etching, and, working under Bléry, he etched the copies from Zeeman that were the foundation of the style of the Paris set. His sensitive, brooding imagination found in the old buildings of Paris themes attuned to his strange, morbid soul. *Le Stryge* (page 136), the etching of the monstrous gargoyle, is the finest expression of the tormented spirit of Meryon. *Le Petit Pont* (page 137), one of his first great plates, with its uncanny vivid light and the dark towers of Notre Dame looming up against the sky, *La Galerie de Notre Dame*, *La Rue des Mauvais Garçons*, sinister in its suggestive terror, all have the expression of his haunted, lonely spirit. How could the lively free line, spontaneously suggestive, express the portentous, tragic power of such a print as *La Morgue* (page 138)? To belittle Meryon's achievements because the rigid quality of his etched line seems, at first sight, to be akin to engraving is neither just nor sound criticism. His line is never mechanical, but pure and true to the character of the themes he chose to depict, and the style he evolved is entirely personal. Through all the great plates he produced, from *Le Petit Pont*, the first of the Paris set, to the *L'Abside de Notre Dame*, a plate which is suffused with radiant sunlight, there is a definite character of genius, sombre indeed, but nevertheless lifting them to the rank of the greatest products of human imagination.

His life was one long record of tragic mental suffering and often dire poverty; he was unable to obtain from his prints—prints for which only the wealthiest collectors can now compete—the bare necessities of life. He died insane in 1868.

Bracquemond stands, together with Meryon, among the leaders of the modern revival of etching. A crafts-

Felix Bracquemond, 1833-1919 man of the highest rank, etching both reproductive and original work, he set a standard of thorough and searching technique that has exercised considerable influence. Among his reproductive work the *Erasmus*, after Holbein, is a classic. His bird pieces are marvellously etched, the *Le Haut d'un Battant de Porte* is a splendid example, and the later *Le Vieux Coq* is a superb print. Among his portraits that of *Legros* (page 141) is well known.

The still-life pieces of Jacquemart are amazing in their extraordinary character and representation of

Jules Jacquemart, 1837-1880 surface and texture. Hamerton, in his appreciation of Jacquemart's work, says: "And as his hand, better than any other human hand, has rendered the hardness of porphyry and the inflexible fragility of porcelain, so also it has most truly interpreted the tender shades and complex delicate lines on which depends the untidiness of the poppy and the beauty of the rose." The series of plates called *Histoire de la Porcelaine* contain some of his finest work, and his reproductive etchings after Vermeer are justly admired both for their extraordinary technical skill and their faithful rendering of all the subtleties of lighting and surface that distinguish the great Dutch Master's paintings. *Ivorie et Céladons* (page 142), *Vase Antique de Porphyre*, and the *Frontispiece* (page 143) are fine examples.

For reliance on a pure clear line, the etchings of Lalanne are rightly admired, and while he had neither

Maxime Lalanne, 1827-1886 the scope nor temperament of his greater contemporaries, his work is always interesting, and shows a complete technical command of the medium. The *Thames at Richmond* and *Les*

FELIX BRACQUEMOND: *Portrait of Alphonse Legros.*
Etching; size of original, $6\frac{5}{8}'' \times 4\frac{1}{2}''$.

From a print in the collection of Mr. Frank L. Emanuel.   141

JULES JACQUEMART: *Ivorie et Céladons*. Etching; size of original, 5″ × 9″.

From a print in the collection of Mr. Frank L. Emanuel.

EAVX·FORTES·MODERNES·
·PVBLIEES·PAR·LA·
SOCIETE·DES·AQVA·FORTISTES·
I.ᵉANNEE·
MDCCCLXIII

JULES JACQUEMART : *Frontispiece*. Etching (G. 331); size
of original, 12¾″ × 9½″.

From a print in the British Museum.   143

MAXIME LALANNE: *Les Acacias.*   Etching (B. 110); size of original, 6″ × 8¾″.

From a print in the collection of Mr. Martin Hardie.

Acacias (page 144) are both excellent examples of his graceful etching of trees and the delicate gradation of his line. *Beuzeval* and *Plage des Vaches Noires, Villers* are admirable etchings; the long stretches of shore receding in subtly suggested perspective are splendidly drawn.

The delightful etching *Aux Environs de Monaco* is an excellent example of the charming art of Appian; it is well composed and freely drawn with a lively, expressive line.

Adolphe Appian, 1819–1898

Manet, the famous painter, etched plates of great interest, and though they are hardly etchings of the highest rank, they have qualities that many technically finer plates conspicuously lack. *The Boy with the Sword* is a good example of his work.

Édouard Manet, 1832–1883

Famous first as a wood engraver, Lepère later etched plates of great vitality. *Amiens: l'Inventaire* is remarkable for the magnificent treatment of the façade of the cathedral and for the vigorous drawing of the riotous crowd in the foreground. Among his landscape etchings which should be studied are *La Petite Mare, Belle Matinée d'Automne, Le Ballon Qui Tombe, Le Pommier renversé* (page 147), and the fine *Ruines du Donjon de Montagne-sur-Sevres*, all good examples. *A Amsterdam*, a subject of a canal and tall buildings, is vigorously treated; and of the Paris subjects *La Seine à l'Embouchure du Canal St. Martin* is remarkable for its variety of interest.

Auguste Lepère, 1849–1918

The great draughtsman, Forain, whose splendid lithographs have been keenly collected for many years, has now by his work as an etcher taken rank with the great modern Masters. No living etcher has his power of selecting the deepest essentials of his subject and stating them with such intensity, and his scriptural subjects have an amazing ardour of utterance unexcelled except by Rembrandt's

Jean Louis Forain, 1852–

L

finest work. *Le Retour de l'Enfant Prodigue* (page 148) is a
noble print of unforced pathos; there is a great dignity
in the simple figure of the father as he grasps the shoulders
of his repentant son. The two figures are set in a simple
open landscape which intensifies the powerful design.
La Fraction du Pain (page 149) is a masterpiece which
owes its power to a conception at once simple and awe-
inspiring. The series of plates of Law-Court subjects
are full of close observation, and the various types
are unerringly depicted—the keen inscrutable lawyers,
the hapless prisoners and all the unfortunate victims of
the law's clutch. *La Sortie de l'Audience* and *Le Prévenu
et l'Enfant* (page 150) are both fine examples. The series
of Lourdes subjects are charged with an intense pity for
the suffering. *L'Imploration* (page 153) is a masterpiece,
with a surging sense of impassioned appeal; its economy
of line is literally amazing.

For sheer original technique and intuitive power, no
modern etcher has excelled Zorn. His prints have a
unique character like nothing produced in
Anders Zorn, etching before them. Roughly bitten, with
1860–1921 a forceful, rugged and vibrating line, to the
lover of the delicate etching they may at first sight
appear repellent. To contrast the wonderful *Renan* with
Rembrandt's *Clement de Jonghe* is an education, and
Zorn does not fail in the tremendous test.

He received his first lessons in etching from his friend,
Axel Haig. Was there ever a greater contrast in the
work of master and pupil? The work of Haig, built up
with meticulous care full of the most intricate detail,
with elaboration carried almost to excess, and Zorn's
trenchant treatment pulsating with vigorous power.
Zorn's portraits show a studied avoidance of the con-
ventional posed effects, and the famous portrait of
Renan represents the finest qualities of his work. *Strindberg* (page 154), *Anatole France*, and *King Oscar*, are
equally fine; and among his portraits of women, the

AUGUSTE LEPÈRE : *Le Pommier renversé*. Etching; size of original,
5¾″ × 7½″.

From a print in the possession of Mr. Martin Hardie.   147

J. L. FORAIN : *Le Retour de l'Enfant Prodigue.* Etching (G. 47) ; size of original
$11\frac{1}{2}'' \times 17\frac{1}{4}''$.

From a print in the collection of Mr. Campbell Dodgson, C.B.E.

J. L. FORAIN: *La Fraction du Pain*. Etching (G. 93); size of original, $11\frac{1}{2}'' \times 10\frac{1}{8}''$.

From a print in the collection of Mr. Campbell Dodgson.

J. L. FORAIN: *Le Prévenu et l'Enfant*.   Etching (G. 52);
size of original, 15¾″ × 11⅞″.

150   From a print in the collection of Mr. Harold J. L. Wright.

beautiful *Mona*, the *Queen Dowager of Sweden*, and the *Mlle. Ema Rassmusson* are thoroughly characteristic. The *Ida* is a remarkable plate with a curiously original effect of lighting from the candle on the ground between the girl's feet as she sits at her work. His treatment of the nude in many prints of bathers he has etched has a healthy, open-air feeling. They are instinct with the vigour of youthful, radiant life. *Storm, The Waltz, The Omnibus* are subject etchings splendid in their verve.

Deeply steeped in sympathetic knowledge of the life of the humbler workers of Paris, Steinlen has produced

Alexandre Théophile Steinlen, 1859- many fine prints drawn with wonderful fidelity. While his line is somewhat coarse and often deeply bitten, and hardly the line of an instinctive etcher as is Forain's, yet the power of his tense, graphic utterance is undeniably masterly.

Such prints as *Le Concert dans La Rue, La Serbe* (page 155)—a plate inspired by the awful tragedy of the great Serbian retreat—and *La Ville Lointaine, Vagabond sous la Neige, Le Coup de Vent*, all attest the power of Steinlen's etching. Among the number of his prints are many printed in colour. The etchings of cats are remarkable for their originality in treatment and keen observation of feline character.

The foremost of the modern Dutchmen who recall the glories of the great seventeenth-century Dutch

Marius Bauer, 1867- School is Marius Bauer, whose etchings of the East are justly admired for their imaginative power. With a free, virile line he suggests the pageantry of Oriental pomp with all its wealth of colour and picturesque costume, and the architectural setting of many of the plates is convincingly drawn. His etchings of Palestine, Egypt, India, and Turkey have all the atmosphere and glamour of the Orient. Among the finest are *A Festival Day at Cairo*, a finely balanced design, *The Holy Ganges* and *Benares*, among the Indian subjects, the long plate *Jerusalem*, and *A Gate* (page 156).

The etchings of the Belgian artist Rops are brilliant in technique and powerful draughtsman-ship, but their erotic nature precludes the general admiration that would otherwise be their due. He used soft ground with fine effect, and his command over drypoint was masterly.

Félicien Rops, 1833-1898

J. L. FORAIN : *L'Imploration.* Etching; size of original, $10\frac{1}{2}'' \times 7\frac{3}{4}''$.

From a print in the collection of Mr. Campbell Dodgson.   153

ANDERS ZORN: *August Strindberg*, 1910. Etching (A. 231); size of original, 11¾″ × 7⅞″.

154   From a print in the collection of Mr. Harold J. L. Wright.

A. T. STEINLEN : *La Serbe*.   Etching; size of original, $11\frac{1}{2}'' \times 19\frac{1}{4}''$.

From a print in the collection of the author.   155

MARIUS BAUER : *A Gate.*   Etching and Drypoint ; size of original, $3\frac{1}{2}'' \times 4\frac{3}{4}''$.

From a print in the collection of Mr. Martin Hardie.

PART IV

DRYPOINT, AQUATINT AND SOFT-GROUND ETCHINGS

FIG. 1.—Reproduction of Drypoint print from a plate showing the bur, which gives the distinctive character to this medium.

FIG. 2.—Reproduction of a print from the same plate, from which the bur has been in parts removed.

ALBRECHT DÜRER: *St. Jerome by the Willow.* Drypoint (B. 59);
size of original, $8\frac{3}{16}'' \times 7\frac{1}{4}''$.

From the print in the British Museum.

REMBRANDT: *Arnold Tholinx*. Drypoint, 1st state (H. 289);
size of original, $7\frac{13}{16}''$ × $5\frac{13}{16}''$.

SIR DAVID WILKIE : *The Lost Receipt*. Drypoint, early state (L. 7) ; size
of original, $5\frac{1}{2}'' \times 6\frac{1}{4}''$.

From a print in the collection of Mr. Harold J. L. Wright.

DRYPOINT, AQUATINT, AND SOFT-GROUND ETCHINGS

DRYPOINT

THIS method should really be called engraving, though it is generally classified with etching. In a pure drypoint the lines are scratched direct upon the plate, either with a sharp steel needle or a diamond mounted in a handle (Fig. 7, page 17), and no acid whatever is necessary. A balanced steel point (Fig. 9, page 17) works perfectly, but any hard piece of steel can be used provided the point is correctly sharpened, either perfectly round or chisel-shaped for strongest work. A good test is to try the point on the thumb-nail; it should scratch with the slightest pressure. A badly-sharpened point will throw up a notched line. The beautiful rich quality in a print from a drypoint is given by the bur, which is a ridge thrown up on one or both sides of the line by the pressure of the point as it cuts into the plate; the greater the pressure the heavier the bur. If the point is held upright the bur will be thrown up on both sides; if held aslant, more will appear on one side. The student will find the diamond point answer splendidly, especially for delicate work; strong bur can also be obtained with it as long as the lines are not crossed. If cross-hatching is resorted to, the diamond is apt to break off in flakes, and it is much safer to use the steel point for very strong work. The burin is often used in conjunction with the dry-point needle, and the contrast given by the clear graved line, with the rich quality of the bur, is often very valuable.

The plate may be prepared with a very thin ground, laid and smoked as for etching, and a tracing transferred for guidance, as it is easier to work upon the smoked ground than the shining surface of the copper. If this method is adopted in preference to working direct upon the clean metal surface, it must always be remembered that the copper itself must be cut into and not merely the ground removed, as in etching. When the work is sufficiently advanced, the ground can be cleaned off and the plate inked up and wiped, and a mixture of tallow and lamp-black is often used for this purpose. The strength of the line and bur can then be gauged and corrections and additions made if necessary. It is inadvisable to wipe the plate too often, as the bur wears all too quickly during the actual printing. If the bur is removed with a scraper, the line will print much the same as a bitten or engraved line (see Fig. 2, page 159). Best copper plates should always be used, and the harder the copper the better. A zinc plate will only yield a very few proofs, as it is so soft a metal. A lightly bitten line is sometimes used as a foundation for a drypoint, and bitten plates are often finished with drypoint, the bur being either removed or left as occasion requires. The contrast of the strong, rich tone held by the bur is often effective against the silvery quality of the fine line left after the bur is removed. Rembrandt frequently mixed etching and drypoint, and the student will find this well exemplified in the *Rembrandt drawing at a Window* (H. 229).

Drypoints require great skill and care in the printing; the bur wears away very rapidly, especially if the plate is wiped entirely with the printing muslin and not with the palm of the hand. Often after about twenty-five prints have been taken the strength of the impression becomes weaker and lacking in depth. The little drypoint (Fig. 1, page 159) was mainly drawn with a steel point; a diamond was used for the delicate lines on the rick, and also for the distance. The second print from the same plate (Fig. 2, page 159) was taken after some of the bur was scraped away, and shows clearly how the print suffers with the removal of the bur.

ANDREW GEDDES : *Peckham Rye.* Drypoint (D. 32) ; size of original, $4\frac{7}{8}'' \times 7\frac{7}{8}''$.

From a print in the Victoria & Albert Museum.

CHARLES JACQUE: *Troupeau de Moutons*. Drypoint (G. 270); size of original,
4″ × 6¼″.

From a print in the possession of Messrs. Colnaghi.

SIR F. SEYMOUR HADEN : *The Little Boat-house*. Drypoint (H. 177); size of original, $5\frac{7}{8}'' \times 8\frac{7}{8}''$.

From a print in the collection of Mr. Martin Hardie.

J. A. McN. WHISTLER : *Axenfeld*.   Drypoint (K. 64) ;
size of original, $8\frac{15}{16}'' \times 5\frac{15}{16}''$.

From a print in the Victoria & Albert Museum.

The earliest pure drypoints were the plates produced by the Master of the Amsterdam Cabinet, the unknown artist of about 1480, the largest collection of whose work is that in the Print Cabinet at Amsterdam. It is certain, however, that the engravers of the sixteenth century used the drypoint in conjunction with the burin. The following are brief notes, with illustrations, on the work of the masters who have used the medium.

Dürer was the first of the masters to make full use **Albrecht Dürer** of the possibilities of the bur in a drypoint, the *St. Jerome by the Willow* (page 160) being a magnificent example.

There is no finer pure drypoint portrait than Rembrandt's *Arnold Tholinx* (H. 289—page 161), in which **Rembrandt** profoundly realised character and structure are expressed with a power that is beyond any master before Rembrandt or since. It is a supreme achievement. Note the directness of the superb drawing, the marvellously rendered light, especially on the face beneath the broad-brimmed hat and the variety of texture suggested; technically it is flawless. The print is extremely rare and can only be seen in museums. Of Rembrandt's pure drypoint landscapes the *Landscape with a Road beside a Canal* (H. 264) is a beautiful example. The values of the sunlight and shadow playing across the road and on the trees and farm-buildings are stated with absolute truth; and the sense of weight and texture throughout is admirable.

Sir David Wilkie's *The Lost Receipt* (page 162), or, as Hamerton describes it, *A Gentleman at his Desk*, **Sir David Wilkie 1785–1841** is a drypoint the student should study. Apart from the extremely fine characterisation of the three figures and the scratching dog, the technical quality of the print is of the highest order.

169

Geddes used drypoint with consummate skill, and the second state of his little plate, now called

Andrew Geddes, 1783–1844 *View of Peckham Rye* (see page 165), is a fine example and carries on the tradition of Rembrandt's drypoint landscapes. The *Portrait of his Mother* is another fine plate. Geddes has been justly described by Wedmore as the link between Rembrandt and the modern masters of drypoint.

Several beautiful drypoints were produced by Charles Jacque, of which *La Vachère*, and *Troupeau de Moutons*

Charles Jacque (page 166) are both prints of great power, showing his perfect command of the medium. The animals are superbly drawn and in design the prints are admirable.

A devout follower of Rembrandt, Haden has exercised very great influence on modern work with the drypoint.

Sir Seymour Haden His best prints are distinguished for their direct simplicity and freedom of line. The lovely *Sunset in Ireland* is a beautiful plate. In an early impression it has a wonderful glowing richness. *Windmill Hill* No. 1 is a print full of sensitive quality, while *The Little Boathouse* (page 167) shows Seymour Haden's method at its best—beautifully balanced design, luminous light and shadow, and direct draughtsmanship making this simple little subject a poem. No student of drypoint should neglect to study closely all the prints of Haden.

Though it is on the beauty of his bitten plates that Whistler's fame chiefly rests, he used the drypoint

James Abbott McNeill Whistler with wonderful effect. *Axenfeld* (page 168) is an arresting drypoint, displaying perhaps more power of characterisation than the master shows in his later work. *Fumette* is another example that shows Whistler's complete command of this medium, whilst *Weary* is one of the most tender and poetical of all his drypoint portraits; the

J. A. McN. WHISTLER : *Annie Haden*. Drypoint
(K. 62) ; size of original, $13\frac{7}{8}'' \times 8\frac{3}{8}''$.

From a print in the Victoria & Albert Museum.   171

ALPHONSE LEGROS: *Le Mur du Presbytère*. Drypoint (No. 335); size of original, 5⅜″ × 7⅜″.

From a print in the collection of Mr. Harold J. L. Wright.

AUGUSTE RODIN: *Victor Hugo*, 1886. Drypoint, 2nd state
(D. 7); size of original, 8¾″ × 6⅞″.

From a print in the British Museum.   173

MUIRHEAD BONE: *Demolition of St. James's Hall (Interior)*, 1906. Drypoint (D. 196); size of original, $15\frac{7}{8}'' \times 11\frac{1}{8}''$.

From a print in the collection of Mr. Campbell Dodgson.

beautiful *Annie Haden* (page 171) was Whistler's own choice as his finest print.

The wide range of Legros' work covers every form of etching, and among his drypoints are many prints of pro-

Alphonse Legros found and simple grandeur. Prof. Hind, in the conclusion of his book on Rembrandt's etchings, says :

> Among modern etchers Legros comes, in my estimation, nearer than Whistler to Rembrandt's genius, on account of the sturdy human sentiment with which his work is inspired.

Prof. Hind's estimate is amply justified by *La Promenade d'un Convalescent ;* for this beautiful print depicts with a quiet reticence the pathetic weakness of the invalid and the solicitude of his companion. Its sentiment is akin to Rembrandt's *Christ healing the Sick*. Of the landscape drypoints *Le Mur du Presbytère* (page 172) is splendidly direct, and is informed with the deep seriousness and austerity which so distinguished all his etched landscapes.

There are but five known drypoints by the great sculptor, Rodin—all distinguished by their sculptural

Auguste Rodin
1840–1917

construction. The *Antonin Prouste*, a profile that is like a lovely medallion, and the portrait of *Victor Hugo* 1886 (page 173), are characteristic examples of his powerful drawing. The graceful *Printemps* is a print of poetical spirit and charm.

Almost the whole of Bone's work on the copper has been done with the drypoint, though he etched a few

Muirhead Bone
1876–

bitten plates very early in his career. He is the master of every phase of drypoint work, and among a prolific output of sustained power he has already produced many plates that justly rank as masterpieces. Such wonderful prints as *The Shot Tower, Rainy Night at Rome, Stirling Castle, Liberty's Clock, Culross Roofs,* and *Walberswick Ferry* are but a few of the prints that have established the fame

of Muirhead Bone. *The Demolition of St. James's Hall,
Interior*, 1906 (page 174), is powerful in design, inspired
in draughtsmanship, and with intricate detail firmly
knit to the beautifully balanced design, is wrought with
amazing skill. *Ayr Prison* (page 177), a somewhat earlier
plate, accepted by many as his masterpiece, has a tremendous tragic intensity entirely in keeping with the character
of the grim old gaol. The student should contrast these
two massive works with the dainty little Venetian plate,
The Giudecca (page 178), or the *Rye from Camber*,
and the beautiful little plate *South Coast* No. 2 (page 179),
and note the range of Bone's achievement. Hamerton, in his hand-book, says : " A man of genius who
loved drypoint and did nothing else would get very fine
effects indeed." Surely Bone has fulfilled this prophecy ?

The more recent work of D. Y. Cameron has almost
entirely consisted of pure drypoint, or etching reinforced
D. Y. Cameron   by drypoint. Distinguished by their deep
spiritual poetry and finely conceived
pattern, his prints take a very important place in modern
work. Among the greatest of his achievements is the
Chimera of Amiens (page 180), though the later Scottish
plates are quite as fine. *Strathearn* is a characteristic
plate full of the knowledge and love of his native landscape, powerful alike in draughtsmanship and expression.
The Esk (page 181), is another drypoint print that is a
memorable work, pure in technique and magnificently
drawn.

Strang's portraits of *Emery Walker* (page 182), and
of *Frederick Goulding*, the famous printer of etchings,
William Strang   reach the highest standard of drypoint,
and are fully worthy to be placed among
the world's finest portrait drypoints. Strang used, with
amazing power and precision, a hook burin which he
invented. The portraits of *J. Craig Annan* and *Thomas
Hardy*, facing left, are characteristic works engraved with
this tool.

MUIRHEAD BONE: *Ayr Prison.* Drypoint (D. 179); size of original, 5″ × 7″.

N

MUIRHEAD BONE: *The Giudecca, Venice.* Drypoint; size of original, 4½″ × 7″.

From a print in the collection of Mr. Campbell Dodgson.

MUIRHEAD BONE: *South Coast*, No. 2. Drypoint; size of original, $4\frac{3}{4}'' \times 8\frac{1}{4}''$.

From a print in the possession of Mr. Campbell Dodgson.

D. Y. CAMERON : *The Chimera of Amiens.* Etching and Drypoint (R. 415); size of original, $9\frac{5}{8}'' \times 7\frac{1}{4}''$.

From a print in the collection of Mr. T. Simpson.

D. Y. CAMERON: *The Esk*.   Drypoint; size of original, $3\frac{31}{32}'' \times 9\frac{5}{8}''$.

From a print in the collection of Mr. Martin Hardie.

W. STRANG : *Portrait of Emery Walker* (No. 473).   Drypoint;
size of original, $14\frac{5}{8}'' \times 9\frac{7}{16}''$.

From a print in the possession of the author.

SIR FRANK SHORT: *A Wintry Blast on the Stourbridge Canal.* Drypoint
(S. 114); size of original, 7″ × 10″.

From a print in the collection of Mr. Harold J. L. Wright.

JAMES McBEY: *The Pianist.* Drypoint; size of original, 7″ × 13″.

From a print in the collection of Mr. T. Simpson.

The *Wintry Blast on the Stourbridge Canal* (page 183) is one of the finest drypoints produced during the

Sir Frank Short last fifty years. The dreariness of the drab, wind-swept and rain-sodden scene is felt and expressed with poetic power and stated with authoritative technique. *Sion House* is another excellent example of Sir Frank Short's skill with the drypoint.

Among the portraits executed by Francis Dodd are many prints of outstanding quality. *The Door-keeper*, the *Bone at the Press*, the *Garden*

Francis Dodd, 1874- *Door*, and the splendid *Epstein* are fine examples of his command over the treatment and resources of drypoint.

The Pianist (page 184) is perhaps the finest drypoint yet produced by McBey; it has superb qualities

James McBey of design and expressive draughtsmanship. *France at her Furnaces* is another splendid drypoint by McBey.

AQUATINT

This much-neglected medium is not sufficiently appreciated either by collectors or students. In capable hands it gives beautiful and expressive results obtained with a simple and easily understood technique. The two principal methods of producing prints in tones are aquatint and mezzotint, and if an example of each is studied side by side the difference in execution will quickly be distinguished. The aquatint, as the name implies, is obtained entirely by the action of the acid biting into the metal through a porous ground, and is composed of simply bitten tones drawn with a brush and varnish on the grounded plate. These may range from a delicate silvery tone to a luminous dark tone according to the length of the immersion in the acid bath. The pure mezzotint is worked without any biting with the acid at all, and its tones are obtained by the working down with the scraper from the deep dark of the rocked plate through half-tones to the highest lights. In aquatint the work is from light to dark, in mezzotint from dark to light, and so the two methods are entirely distinct, but while the aquatint cannot command the strong dark tones or the subtle gradations of a mezzotint, the qualities obtained by fine draughtsmanship and correct relation of the bitten juxtaposed tones are sufficient in themselves without any striving to emulate the inherent qualities of the mezzotint.

The credit for the discovery of aquatint has generally been given to Jean-Baptiste Le Prince. Prof. A. M. Hind, in *The Print Collector's Quarterly* for December 1921, conclusively proves that though Le Prince perfected the use of the dust ground, he was certainly not the first engraver to work with the medium. An examination of the prints by Van de Velde, William Sherwin, Gerhard Janssen, and Paul Burdett, which Professor Hind cites, will quickly convince any etcher with a good working knowledge of the character of aquatint grounds that the hitherto accepted history of the origin of the process is entirely wrong. Malcolm Salaman, in his book *Old English Mezzotints*, published in 1910, also points out the use of aquatint in Sherwin's print of *Catherine, Queen of Charles II.*, and in Jan Van de Velde's curious print of *Oliver Cromwell*. The same great authority also wrote on this question in the introductory chapter, pages 25 and 26, of *French Colour Prints*, 1913, and in the chapter on aquatint in the *Print Collector's Handbook*, 1912.

Paul Sandby in 1775 invented what is known as the spirit ground in aquatint, which almost entirely superseded the dust-ground method; its greater luminosity and quality of tone quickly appealed to the aquatinters of the period. The work of William Daniel, F. C. Lewis, and Harraden, who aquatinted some of Girtin's soft-ground etchings, are good examples of the use of the medium.

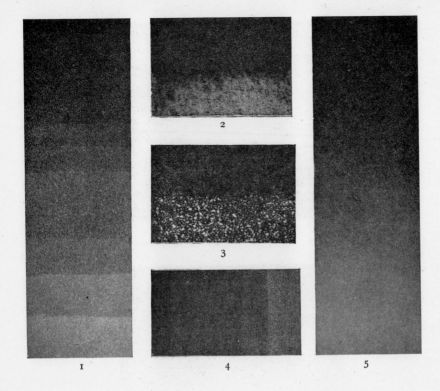

1
2
3
4
5

DUST GROUNDS AND SAND-PAPER GROUND

No. 1.—Example of bitten tones, each successive stopping out being plainly shown. Compare with No. 5.

No. 2.—Example of the ground breaking up through overbiting; the top portion was stopped out and the lower overbitten.

No. 3.—A very coarse ground was first laid by shaking resin through a piece of fine muslin, and after the plate was bitten and a proof taken, a fine ground was laid over the coarse ground and the top portion bitten again.

No. 4.—An example of sand paper ground.

No. 5.—An example of a graduated tone attained by lowering the plate very slowly into the acid. The fine ground is resin dust and was laid in a fan box; the plate was placed in the box for one and a half minutes and then taken out and the fan revolved again. It was twice replaced in the box for a minute each time, making a total of three and a half minutes.

I

2

No. 1.—An example of a fine spirit-ground. The solution was much more diluted than for No. 2.

No. 2.—An example of a coarse spirit-ground laid with a strong solution of resin in spirits of wine.

The invention of lithography caused the process to become almost entirely neglected until Sir Frank Short revived its practice with a conception of its possibilities as an original art entirely beyond the scope of the earlier aquatinters.

The two methods of laying aquatint grounds are : (1) the Dust ground, (2) the Spirit ground.

Very finely powdered resin or asphaltum form the dust ground; resin gives a very good ground, but

Dust Grounds asphaltum is the best dust for very fine grounds. A large box, not less than from two to three feet high is used, having near the bottom a door just high enough to allow the plate to be comfortably slipped in and out of the box, and this door is hinged to the bottom, fits very tightly, and extends the whole width of the box. The resin or asphaltum is placed in the bottom of the box and the air inside violently disturbed until the interior is filled with a dense cloud of dust.

This cloud can be raised in several ways. The most usual pattern of box contains at the bottom a revolving fan which is whirled round by a handle outside the box. In another pattern the whole box rotates. A more primitive method, though quite an effective one, is to use a large pair of bellows, the nozzle of which is fitted into a hole in the side of the box. When the box is at rest the dust should be allowed to settle for a few seconds; the plate may then be slipped inside and left resting on a rack-tray, the door being gently closed. This rack-tray is used to allow the dust to pass through the rails to the bottom of the box, for if the tray were solid it would collect all the dust. The plate is always put on a piece of stiff paper or cardboard at least one inch larger all round than the plate. If this is not done the density of the ground, near the edges of the plate, will be thinner than the centre. Myriads of minute specks of the dust will settle on the plate, and the density of the ground can be regulated by the time the plate is left in the box. If a very coarse ground is wanted (Fig. 3, page 187) the plate should be placed inside the box directly the fan ceases revolving, as the heaviest specks of dust settle first. Fig. 1, page 187, shows a print from a plate which was placed in the box three times for a minute each time. When the plate is finally taken out of the box it is covered with a thick layer of the dust and is ready for fixing.

The grounded plate is placed on the heater or clasped with a hand-vice and held over a Bunsen burner, and the change of colour that occurs when the dust melts must be closely observed. It will run across the surface of the plate very quickly, the resin changing from a creamy white to a faint amber spread over the copper colour, and the brown asphaltum will change to a bluish tint. The plate must be removed directly the change occurs, the back coated with varnish and the plate allowed to cool. Great care needs to be taken to avoid burning the ground, for when this mistake is made the biting will be very irregular. Greater heat is required to melt asphaltum than resin, and it should be held over the Bunsen burner.

The plate, at any rate on one side, should be at least half an inch larger than the actual size of the drawing, for if a little ground is removed from this spare slip with turpentine and a warm rag after each biting, the strength of the tones can be gauged with fair accuracy. The key of tones given by the unwanted slip is most useful, and the unwanted portion can be quickly removed by the guillotine when the plate is completed.

The success of an aquatint, apart from the biting, depends entirely on the drawing of the tones with the brush charged with stopping-out varnish. The varnish works better if used in different consistencies, for if it is too fluid, it will run between the specks of the ground and spread beyond the border of the desired tone; it is

FRANCISCO GOYA: *Por Que Fue Sensible*. Aquatint
(H. 32); size of original, 8½″ × 6″.

From a print in the collection of Mr. Con. H. Lomax. 191

EUGÈNE DELACROIX: *The Blacksmith.* Aquatint
(D. 19); size of original, $6\frac{3}{8}'' \times 3\frac{7}{8}''$.

192   From a print in the collection of Mr. Harold J. L. Wright.

as well to pour a little of the varnish into a saucer and allow it to thicken slightly—a small palette is very useful. Crisp touches can be obtained with thicker varnish. If very fine lines are needed the work can be drawn with a fine brush, using a thick solution of sugar dissolved in water and coloured black. The plate is then varnished over, and when the varnish is " tacky " if the plate is placed in water the sugar will dissolve and come away, leaving the lines open to the action of the acid when the plate is bitten in the usual way.

Both the nitric, weaker than for biting line, and the Dutch bath can be used, though it is difficult to give **Biting** exact times for biting. The tones are studied carefully before the biting is started, and the student needs to have a fixed idea of how many stoppings out he will require. Any pure whites required are painted out first, and then the problem is to bite the darker tones correctly one after another, stopping out as the work progresses, until finally only the very darkest tones remain unpainted with the varnish. After this last and darkest tone is bitten the ground should be removed and a proof taken (Fig. 1, page 187). The student will note that aquatint bites very rapidly as compared with etching.

The key slip should be frequently examined during the process of the biting, and care must be taken not to over-bite. In contrast with the too heavy black lines which occur when an etching is over-bitten, in an over-bitten aquatint the ground will break away entirely owing to the acid eating under the copper covered by the tiny specks of resin. If this happens the last tones will print a dismal grey, as is seen in Fig. 2, page 187. New grounds can be laid for corrections and additions, but a very much worked plate soon shows signs of fumbling, and it is much better to use as few grounds as possible. The scraper and the burnisher can be used to merge the edges of the bitten tones, but the less inter-

o

ference with the tones the better; for an aquatint
should stand by the inherent quality and beauty of the
process, and not be pushed into the method of mezzotint and become what Mr. Malcolm Salaman fittingly
describes as a " mongrel mezzotint." If the biting is
correctly related, the value of the tones will be so just
that burnishing or scraping should hardly be needed.

The spirit ground is composed of resin or asphaltum dissolved in spirits of wine or pure alcohol, and
Spirit Ground   when the solution is poured over the
plate the evaporation of the spirit leaves
the resin in innumerable minute grains covering the
surface of the plate. These resist the action of the
acid which attacks the tiny channels of unprotected
metal, so forming the bitten tones. To prepare the
solution, five ounces of finely-ground resin is dissolved in
a pint of spirit of wine. The bottle is shaken several
times during the day and then left for another twenty-
four hours to allow the impurities to settle. The solution
prepared will be much too strong, and a fresh bottle is
used, and a mixture of one-third of the solution to two-
thirds of spirit of wine mixed together. If a very fine
ground is wanted (Fig. 1, page 188) the second
solution is again diluted, for the stronger the solution of
resin the larger will be the granulation and the coarser
the ground (Fig. 2, page 188).

To lay the ground, the plate is cleaned with whitening
and ammonia, and dried; the solution is then poured over
the plate, which is held slightly inclined over a trough or
dish, the lower edge being wiped from time to time to
remove the liquid that gathers there. The plate must
not be held at too steep an angle or the granulation will
not be round but elongated. If, however, this longer
grain is wanted, as it might be, the plate is tilted. It is
of advantage to gently sway the plate with a circular
motion while the ground is drying. The great enemy to
successful spirit ground is dust, and, as soon as the grains

SIR FRANK SHORT : *A Span of Old Battersea Bridge*. Aquatint (S. 226) ; size
of original, $7\frac{1}{2}'' \times 11\frac{5}{8}''$.

From a print in the possession of Messrs. Colnaghi.

SIR FRANK SHORT: *Morning Haze, Chichester Harbour*. Aquatint; size of
original, 13⅝″ × 9⅜″.

From a print in the collection of the author.

begin to settle, the plate is laid flat and covered by a board raised well above it. The solution that runs off into the trough or dish is not poured back into the unused solution before it has been filtered through a funnel with a fine-meshed rag or silk, for it is certain to collect dust.

Laying a spirit ground is very much a gamble, for weather conditions affect the process greatly. If the ground is attempted in very hot weather, or in a cold room during frost, it refuses to granulate. The best time to try is early morning on a dry day with a moderate temperature. The biting of the tones can be proceeded with in exactly the same way as described with the dust ground. The experienced etcher will find by practice that he can use a feather or brush charged with the acid and bite portions of the plate to obtain gradations. The student must remember that aquatint-grounded plates bite much quicker than hard ground plates, and fifteen to twenty minutes in the bath suffices to complete the biting. If it be found after the first print has been taken that further darker tones are required, another ground can be laid over the old work, when it is advisable to use a coarser ground.

EXAMPLES OF FAMOUS AQUATINTS

The Spanish master used the dust-ground aquatint with miraculous skill in the print called *Por Que Fue Sensible* (page 191) from *Los Caprichos*.
Goya Not a single hard or soft ground etched line is used ! Contrary to Goya's practice of reinforcing his bitten-line etchings with strong contrasts of light and shadow obtained with aquatint, this print is drawn entirely with brush and varnish. Examine closely the drawing in the folds of the dress, the head and the feet. The simplicity and directness of the bitten tones convey all the suggestion of space and plane, and the whole

print is charged with a tragic intensity that makes it unique among pure aquatints. Mr. Walter Sickert, writing of this print in an interesting and provocative article in the *Burlington Magazine*, September 1915, says : " This plate is a meeting-place of supreme passion, supreme skill, and supreme luck, the sort of conjuncture that happens perhaps once in a century." The plate seems little touched after biting, and technically is a pure triumph.

In the *Blacksmith* (page 192) Delacroix worked with a spirit ground and produced one of the marvels **Eugène** of aquatint. The complicated tones of **Delacroix,** the glowing metal and the dark blacksmith **1798–1863** and his assistant at the bellows are marvellously rendered. The drawing with the brush is superbly managed. There is a working proof in the British Museum with a border which shows how carefully Delacroix watched the biting of his plate.

Battersea Bridge (page 195), by Sir Frank Short, was worked with two grounds, a dust ground being used for **Sir Frank Short** the timbers of the old wooden bridge and the foreground, and a spirit ground for the distance seen through the span of the bridge. The biting is beautifully managed and the different grains of the two grounds admirably used for contrast in textures. This plate is justly esteemed as one of the finest aquatints ever produced. *Sunrise over Whitby Scaur* and *Dawn* are other fine aquatints which reach heights unexplored by his predecessors. His latest aquatint, *Morning Haze in Chichester Harbour* (page 196), is a beautiful, delicately bitten plate, most poetical in conception and masterly in treatment.

Sand-paper Aquatint

This method of producing bitten tones is made by placing a sheet of fine sand or glass paper face downwards over an ordinary wax-grounded plate, and passing the plate with the blankets over it two or three times through the press, using a fresh piece of sand-paper each time. The pressure causes the grains of sand to perforate the wax in innumerable small holes, forming a ground somewhat similar to a resin ground. Sand-paper of varying degrees of coarseness can be used to get a variety of texture. The method of working is precisely the same as when using a dust or spirit ground, the tones being gained by stopping out with the brush and varnish and biting with the acid (Fig. 4, page 187). This method will not produce quite the depth of tone that can be obtained by the dust or spirit ground, and lacks the silvery quality that distinguishes pure aquatint. Legros used this method in his great print called *The Dying Vagabond* (page 107).

Soft-ground Etching

By the use of soft-ground, prints are produced giving a quality closely akin to a pencil or chalk drawing, and the method of biting followed is exactly similar to ordinary etching, but the line resulting from the process is much wider. Soft-ground was very largely used for reproducing drawings before the advent of lithography, which by its greater certainty quickly drove the more laborious process into disfavour.

Soft-ground is composed of equal quantities of ordinary etching ground and tallow melted together. It requires to be kept in a small silk bag and laid on the plate with a dabber exactly as for an ordinary ground but with less heat, and then smoked; a little less tallow is needed in the summer. A separate dabber is always used; the hard-ground dabber will often spoil the ground. Care has to be taken not to touch the ground with the fingers, and it is advisable to use a hand-rest during the working. A sheet of grained paper (smooth paper will give no result whatever, but strong tissue-paper is excellent) is damped, stretched over the surface of the ground, gummed or glued on to the back of the plate and allowed to dry.

This is the safest method to use, but tracing paper can be used for the drawing, which is pinned down over the plate, and papers of various grains and textures placed under the tracing paper next to the ground; thus a variety of quality of line can be obtained. The design is drawn upon the paper with a pencil and the pressure varied according to the strength of line desired. The ground will be lifted from the plate, as it clings to the back of the paper, exposing the copper where the lines have been drawn. When the drawing is completed the paper is carefully removed and the plate bitten. While in the acid bath the plate must be closely watched for foul-biting, often a great trouble with soft-ground, and for this reason nitric acid is always used, and it is always advisable to paint over with stopping-out varnish all large plain surfaces. The bubbles that form during the biting must be gently " tickled " off and the feather never allowed to brush the ground.

EXAMPLES OF FINE SOFT-GROUND ETCHINGS

Soft-ground was largely used, both alone and with aquatint tones, in the eighteenth and nineteenth centuries. There are some beautiful plates by Gainsborough, of which *The Watering-Place* is a typical example, and Rowlandson also used the medium with great success. The beautiful series of *Views of Paris* by Thomas Girtin are among the finest prints ever made with soft-ground, and the set in the Print Room of the British Museum should be studied to appreciate how, in the hands of a master, this neglected process may convey the subtlest sense of distance. The plate called *Water Works at Marli* is a fine example. Turner also used soft-ground in a few of the *Liber Studiorum* plates, notably in the beautiful

JOHN CROME: *Trees on a Bank by the Roadside.* Soft-ground Etching (T. 34);
size of original, $6\frac{3}{8}'' \times 9\frac{1}{8}''$.

From a print in the British Museum.

JOHN SELL COTMAN: *Parsons Bridge.* Soft-ground
Etching (P. 306); size of original, $6\frac{7}{8}'' \times 4\frac{7}{8}''$.

From a print in the collection of the author.

Calm, the first state of which is pure soft-ground and is exquisite.

The soft-ground etchings of Crome are excellent examples of the use of the medium. *The Trees on a Bank by the Roadside* (page 201) is especially fine; it is strongly bitten, very happy in composition and has a luminous atmospheric effect. *The Sketch of a Tree Trunk* and *Hoveton St. Peter* are other good examples.

John Sell Cotman (1782–1842) produced very beautiful soft-ground etchings, and in his *Liber Studiorum* will be found some of the finest examples of the process, which have much of the quality of his incomparable drawings.

A Study, Liber Studiorum No. 17, and *Parsons Bridge* (page 202), are good examples of his fine design, superb draughtsmanship and command of the medium. *Carnarvon Castle, Postwick Grove, Twickenham* and *Bambro' Castle* are other famous prints of his in this medium. *Gathering the Flock on Maxwell Bank,* by Sir Frank Short, is another example of masterly treatment of soft-ground.

PART V
PRINTING, MOUNTING, AND THE CARE OF PRINTS

FIG. 1.—Example of vilely faked printing.

FIG. 2.—Example of straightforward printing.

PRINTING, MOUNTING, AND THE CARE OF PRINTS

PRINTING, PAPER, ETC.

AFTER surmounting all the difficulties of etching the plate, there is the final task of printing or proving, a process at once most fascinating and tantalising. The beginner needs to obtain the help of a competent printer to pull the first proofs, for, however well the mere description of printing may be studied and absorbed, to print at all satisfactorily, long practice, experience and constant experiment are necessary.

I have always advised students to print their own plates : their ideal should be to etch a good plate and then print it to the utmost advantage themselves—printing cleanly and truly, the quality of the line being considered before everything. The line will never be improved if it is smothered with ink left on the surface of the plate, as is the fashion with many etchers to-day. Reproductions are shown (Figs. 1 and 2, page 206) of proofs from the same etching: Fig. 1 shows as many sins of commission as I was able to compass on the plate; the sky is faked, the trees are over-printed, and a spurious light is wiped out on the water; Fig. 2 is a straightforward print, and that is the best type of printing. The student will find this pay best in the long run. Sympathetic printing is one thing, to over-print the plate with dragged muslin or " retroussage " is another.

A too clean proof may be dry and dull as a visiting card, but an inky proof is the devil's own visiting card.

The preparation of ink is very important. So much

can be done with variations of colour, strength and
Ink consistency that there is unending interest
in experimenting. All plates will not print
well with the same kind of ink, and it is necessary for
the printer to mix his ink according to the strength of
the bitten line or bur of the drypoint.

Burnt linseed oil is used and is made in three consistencies—thick, medium, and thin. The oil is prepared
Oils by first boiling the linseed oil in a cauldron
and then setting fire to it. It is continu-
ously stirred, and the longer it is allowed to burn, the
thicker and more like varnish it becomes.

Good Frankfurt Black is the foundation of most inks,
and the best should always be used, for the cheaper
Pigments kinds are gritty and a plentiful crop of
scratches may result from using them.
Heavy and Light French Blacks are very good, and
especially a black called Bougou, which is prepared
from the dregs of wine-presses. Burnt Umber of the
drop variety is the best brown, though Japanese Brown
and Red are very useful. Frankfurt Black, Heavy
French and a little burnt Umber will give an ink with
good body. Forcing Black is useful, especially for an
under-bitten plate, though it is as well to avoid excessive
use of it. Earth colours only are used. Roman Ochre
is useful and also Burnt Sienna, though it is rather hot
in colour. Brown ink sets very quickly, but black ink
will keep a few days if it is put in a tin.

The ink is well ground with a muller on a slab (an
old lithographic stone is excellent for the purpose), and
a little extra work when grinding will always ward off
those insidious scratches. Ready-made inks can be
obtained in tubes, but the self-prepared inks are advisable.

If a slight surface tone is wanted, the ink should be
sloppy and mixed with thin oil. Thick ink mixed with
thin oil will give a brilliant proof, and if the plate is
heavily bitten a stiff ink is best.

The dabber on which the ink is spread and applied
to the plate is made of cloth covered with a stocking;
great care should be taken to scrape off the ink after
the printing is finished, for if this is not done the dabber
will get hard and useless and must be re-covered.

The paper is damped before it is used, sponged
lightly, and then carefully laid out between two sheets
of zinc or glass. It is pressed out quite
Paper   flat, and all crinkles and rucks smoothed
out. If possible, the paper is given twenty-four hours,
or at least a night's damping down, before it is used for
printing. Good hand-made paper gives the best results,
and many different qualities can be obtained; indeed
there is a great fascination in choosing paper, and old
pure linen paper is eagerly sought after. Hunts in out-
of-the-way shops and places may often yield a prize in
the shape of an old book with fly-leaves unprinted on
with type, or, better still, old albums. Japanese paper
is also largely used and gives beautiful impressions.
The only objection to it is that its surface is easily rubbed
up if badly handled. A piece of damped plate paper
should always be used as backing to the Japanese paper.

Heavily sized paper should be avoided, as it hardens
the blankets. China paper and India paper are both
good, especially the first, which, with a good rich black
ink, gives a very fine print. It is necessary to use backing
with these papers. Specks, which often mar the surface
of paper, should be carefully removed with tweezers.

The ink being ready, just enough to cover well the
surface of the plate is spread over the surface of the
dabber with a broad palette knife. The
Taking Proofs   plate is then placed on the heater, which
is made just warm enough for the plate to receive the
ink easily. The dabber is then rocked backwards and
forwards across the plate with a steady downward
pressure, driving the ink well into the lines. Only
sufficient ink is needed; too much will spoil the printing

P

muslin. The inked plate is then removed to the jigger and the ink wiped off the surface with the printing muslin.

The ink is removed gradually, and usually two pads of muslin are used, the first taking most of the ink off with fairly strong sweeps up and across the plate, while the second is used to finish the wiping, with a more or less circular motion, and, of course, is kept much the cleaner pad of the two.

The muslin is folded into a flat pad with no seams on the bottom, and the wiping is done with a perfectly flat motion, pressing down the whole time, the aim of the printer being to drive the ink into the lines and at the same time to remove it from the plain surface of the plate. If the muslin pad is used with a scooping action the ink will be taken out of the lines, and a weak impression will be the result when the plate is printed.

Plates are often hand-wiped with the palm of the hand—covered with a film of ink and whitening—and this often gives the best result, if the method is properly used, the print being clean yet sympathetic. After wiping, the plate is warmed again and a piece of very soft muslin lightly run across the plate, bringing the ink up over the edges of the sunken lines and imparting a softness to the print. It is very easy to overdo this " retroussage," and it needs to be used very sparingly.

The bevelled edges of the plate are now well cleaned with a rag and the plate is ready for printing, and before it gets quite cold it should be laid on the zinc bed of the press. The back of the plate must be perfectly clean, for if spots of dry ink or hard varnish are allowed to remain, the pressure of the rollers will cause nasty raised spots on the surface of the plate.

The blankets are always placed in the press before the printing is commenced, and a little care in getting them square to the sides of the press, and also with

the ends slightly overlapping, is necessary. Five thick-
nesses of blanket are used, two next to the print of a
close texture called fronting, such as is used for billiard-
tables, and three of a much thicker quality called swan-
skin above the fronting. These blankets require to be
carefully looked after and never left in the press after
the printing is finished, for they harden and do not
work so well after such bad treatment. The paper,
which is lightly brushed to remove any dust or pieces
that may spoil the print, is then laid over the plate and
the blankets placed evenly down over the paper. The
plate is then passed through the rollers of the press
and the print removed by carefully lifting the two corners
and peeling the paper from the plate. If the paper
sticks to the plate and this trouble is perceived in time
before the proof is ruined, both the plate and the paper
are carefully lifted on to the heater and the warmth
will usually release the paper. When the printing is
finished the plate is carefully cleaned with turpentine
and rag, and, if it is not to be used again for some time,
it should be warmed and covered with a coating of
beeswax. The zinc bed-plate of the press is kept scrupulously clean and wiped frequently with turpentine and
a rag.

The pressure of the press has to be perfectly regulated, and experience will quickly teach this; in a good
print the lines of ink stand up in relief and there is a
gloss over the surface of the print. Too much pressure
must be avoided as well as too little. In the first case
the great difficulty when turning the press will tell the
student he has over-tightened his press, while with
the second fault the weak impression with grey and
faint lines will quickly show the need of more pressure.
Unequal pressure is usually a trouble until the press is
thoroughly understood. This is due to one side of the
press not being keyed as tightly as the other. Over-
pressure will often cut the paper and sometimes damage

the blankets, and the thickness of the plate should always be allowed for.

When the print is taken from the press, it is either stretched out on a board by pasting the edges, or, better still, allowed to dry, and some days afterwards damped again, and flattened out under pressure. The old printers used to peg the proofs up on lines like clothes, and old prints of printing shops show hundreds of them thus drying. Of course the latter process preserves the deckle edge of the paper, and a screw linen-press is excellent for flattening prints out. The prints are damped and placed between sheets of plate-paper or paste-board, and the plate-papers are changed every twenty-four hours until the prints are perfectly dry and flat. The plate-paper and paste-board should be dried in the air before being used again.

Some further hints on printing may be found useful to the student. The hands become very grimed with ink, and the best way to remove the ink is to pour some sperm oil into the palms and rub the hands well together, afterwards washing the oil away with warm water and soap. When the student is printing without help, a small doubled tab of paper will be found useful to handle the paper with, so avoiding finger and thumb prints around the border. The blankets, after the printing is finished, are always hung up to dry, and if they become hard with constant use, they should be washed and well rinsed to get rid of any soap that may tend to harden the surface. The stone, on which the ink is mixed, and the muller are cleaned with a rag and turpentine, and the surfaces of the heater, jigger and bed of the press are always kept scrupulously clean with a rag and turpentine.

A counterproof of any etching can be taken by placing a fresh clean sheet of damped paper over the impression with the ink still wet and pulling the two face together through the press. This counterproof will enable the etcher to work without the looking-glass, but it will, of course, be weaker than the first print and is only useful as a guide to drawing.

MOUNTING AND CARE OF PRINTS

To mount prints properly and to ensure that they show to the best advantage is a comparatively simple matter, though the appearance of many prints is spoilt by disproportionate mounts and frames of bad design. After the prints have been pressed or stretched carefully (and it should be remembered that a wrinkled print is very unsightly), they are hinged on to the back mount. Under no circumstances should they be pasted down, for many a print restorer has anathematised the foolish practice, which sometimes entirely ruins prints. The card at the back of the mount should be of the best quality white cardboard, and never straw-board, which will stain the print horribly if damp reaches it. The front mount requires to be of such size as to give a border of sufficient width to ensure a good proportion to the print, and a little more space is always given to the bottom border. A print placed plumb in the centre of the mount has a curious effect of slipping down out of the mount. The border should not be too small, for that fault will give the effect of dwarfing and cramping the print, and it certainly should not be of too great a width, for the print then assumes the look of a postage stamp. It is advisable to keep prints in mounts of standard size, both for keeping them in solander boxes, which are invaluable to the collector, and also for framing. If the frames are made with movable backs the prints can be readily changed from time to time.

Frames should be of a simple character; oak and walnut are the best woods to use, and if made with good workmanship they need not be at all heavy. Solander boxes are better than portfolios for keeping prints free from dust, and the greatest care should be taken to ensure that they are placed in perfectly dry surroundings, for damp is the arch-enemy of the good condition of prints. The frequent airing of the prints comes automatically with good connoisseurship, and if the glass of a frame be accidentally cracked, the accident should be attended to at once, and not left till the dust penetrates through the cracks in the glass and causes lines to appear on the print.

Cleaning should never be attempted. It is the province of the expert, and many fine prints have been hopelessly ruined by amateur efforts at restoration.

PART VI

CONCLUSION

CONCLUSION

" *Few have been taught to any purpose who have not been their own teachers.*"—SIR JOSHUA REYNOLDS, *Discourses on Painting*.

I HAVE described, as well as I am able, the various processes through which the etcher endeavours to express the degree of talent and inspiration with which he is endowed. Etching is not an art that can be lightly engaged in, the many and varying technicalities requiring much study and labour. With the statement, " The test of mastery is the ability to canalise sustained enthusiasm," Walter Sickert has succinctly stated the greatest need of the budding etcher. No student who attempts to evade the difficulties of the craft by trick will go far, and the collector, too, should learn to differentiate between an honest technique which is the basis of all great work in any art, and a tricky evasion of its difficulties.

From the very first experimental plate the young etcher should begin to equip himself with a technique gathered with patience, and therefore with surety, and a clear knowledge of the province and limitations of the medium. Draughtsmanship deeply felt and finely expressed is the greatest essential in the equipment of the etcher. The aim should be not for mere accurate representation, which can be acquired by industry and care, but for finely felt and sincere drawing expressing an individual outlook, a gift that is not often bestowed. All the masters, " the strong men," as Millet loved to call them, were great draughtsmen, and there is no greater test of draughtsmanship than etching. Whether the theme be stated simply with an extreme economy of

217

line, as in Forain's *L'Imploration*, or with great detail
as in Muirhead Bone's *Great Gantry*, the suggestive
quality and selection of line rules all the merit of etched
work, for either its power succeeds and convinces, or it
clouds and confuses the intention.   Fussy, overworked
detail in a print is like the distressing verbiage of the bore
who spoils a good story with his own unnecessary inter-
polations.

Many cleverly drawn, perfectly bitten and printed
plates are to be found everywhere, but the few that
enchain the abiding interest are the work of more than
the mere technician, virtuoso though he be.   I know no
better way to convey this last point than to give a
quotation from George Clausen's *Lectures on Painting* :

> It seems as if in the artist's mind the desire to
> express his subject and the desire to display his skill
> are conflicting tendencies.   When these are in
> perfect balance we get the finest work.   When the
> desire for expression is the stronger we get sincere
> and beautiful, but imperfect and immature work,
> as in the case of the early Primitives.   But when the
> desire for the display of skill is the stronger, we get
> cleverness, affectation, and decadence.

Collections such as those in the British Museum
Print-room and in the Victoria and Albert Museum are
for the use of students and collectors, but are all too little
used by them, I am afraid; and, for those who cannot
avail themselves of national collections, fine reproductions of many of the greatest masterpieces of etching
can be obtained at a comparatively modest cost.   That
close and intelligent study of the great work of the masters
is of undoubted use to the student can hardly be gainsaid ;
but the delicate flower of self-expression, so hard to rear
and often so easily smothered by well-meaning teachers,
should be carefully nurtured.   To the real teacher, even
a rebellious student, trying to express his own ideas,

should be a more precious possession than a hundred sycophantic followers, apishly repeating every little mannerism of their master. Millet wrote to Sensier these words :

Men of genius are gifted with a sort of divining-rod. Some discover in Nature this, others that, according to their kind of scent. Their productions assure you that he who finds is formed to find; but it is funny to see how, when the treasure is unearthed, people come for ages to scratch at the same hole.

PART VII

A BIBLIOGRAPHY OF WORKS ON ETCHING AND ETCHERS

A BIBLIOGRAPHY OF
WORKS ON ETCHING AND ETCHERS

General Works on Etching

Alken, Henry.	*Art and Practice of Etching.* London, 1849.
Ashley, Alfred.	*The Art of Etching on Copper.* London, 1849 and 1851.
Barnard, Osbert H.	*The Clichés-Verre of the Barbizon School.* Print Coll. Quarterly, Vol. IX., 1922.
Binyon, Laurence.	*Dutch Etchers of the Seventeenth Century.* The Portfolio, London, 1895.
Bosse, Abraham.	*Traicté des manières de graver.* Paris, 1645, 1701.
Bourcard, Gustave.	*Les Estampes du Dix-huitième Siècle.* Paris, 1885.
,, ,,	*Graveurs et Gravures.* Paris, 1910.
Bradley, W. A.	*Some French Etchers and Sonneteers.* Print Coll. Quarterly, Vol. IV., 1914.
,, ,,	*The Etching of Figures.* Chicago Soc. of Etchers, 1915.
,, ,,	*Dutch Landscape Etchers of the Seventeenth Century.* New Haven, U.S.A., 1918.
Carrington, Fitzroy.	*Prints and their Makers.* London, 1913.
,, ,,	*Engravers and Etchers* (Scannon Lectures). Chicago, 1917.
Chattock, R. S.	*Practical Notes on Etching.* London, 1883.
Courboin, F.	*Graveurs et Marchands d'Estampes au XVIII. Siècle.* Paris, 1914.
Delaborde, Henri.	*Engraving, its Origin, Processes and History.* London, 1886.
Dossie, R.	*The Handmaid to the Arts.* 2 vols. London, 1758.
Fagan, Louis.	*Collector's Marks.* London, 1883.
Faithorne, W.	*The Art of Graving and Etching, wherein is expressed the true way of graving in copper,* 1662. 2nd ed. London, 1702.
Fielding, T. H.	*Art of Engraving.* London, 1844.

Green, J. H. *The Complete Aquatinter.* London, 1801.

Haden, Arthur. *Chats on Old Prints.* London, 1906; 2nd ed., 1909.

Haden, Sir Francis Seymour. *About Etching.* London, 1878.

„   „ *The Art of the Painter-etcher.* London, 1890.

„   „ *The Relative Claims of Etching and Engraving to Rank as Fine Arts.* Soc. of Arts. London, 1883.

Hamerton, P. G. *Etching and Etchers.* London, 2nd ed., 1868; 3rd ed., 1880.

„   „ *The Graphic Arts.* London, 1882.

„   „ *The Etcher's Hand-book.* London, 1st ed., 1871; 2nd ed., 1875.

„   „ *Landscape.* London, 1885.

Hardie, Martin. *British School of Etching.* (Print Collectors' Club : Inaugural Lecture.) London, 1922.

Hassell, John. *Graphic Delineation : a Practical Treatise on the Art of Etching.* London, 1826.

Herkomer, Sir Hubert. *Etching and Mezzotint Engraving.* London, 1892.

Hind, A. M. *Short History of Engraving and Etching,* with full bibliography, London, 1908. 2nd ed., 1911.

„   „ *Notes on History of Soft-Ground Etching and Aquatint.* Print Coll. Quarterly, Vol. VIII., 1921.

„   „ *Guide to the Processes and Schools of Engraving.* British Museum. London, 1914.

„   „ *A History of Engraving and Etching from the Fifteenth Century to the year 1914.* Being 3rd ed. of Short Hist. of Engraving, etc. London, 1922.

Hitchcock, J. R. W. *Etching in America.* New York, 1886.

Holme, Charles. *Modern Etching and Engraving.* The Studio, London. 1902.

„   „ *Modern Etching and Mezzotint.* The Studio, London, 1913.

Huband, W. *Critical and Familiar Notices on the Art of Etching.* Dublin, 1810; 2nd ed., 1813.

Hubbard, E. Hesketh.	*On Making and Collecting Etchings.* London, 1920.
Jaques, B. C.	*Concerning Etchings.* Chicago, 1913.
Kepple, Frederick.	*The Golden Age of Engraving.* New York, 1910.
Koehler, S. R.	*Etching : an Outline of its Technical Processes and its History.* New York. 1885.
,, ,,	*American Etchers.* Amer. Art Review, 1880–1881.
Kristeller, Paul.	*Kupferstich and Holzschnitt.* 3rd ed. Berlin, 1921.
Lalanne, Maxime.	*Traité de la Gravure à l'Eau-Forte,* 1866. Paris, 1878. American translation : Boston, 1880.
Lippmann, F.	*History of Engraving and Etching,* 1906. Translated from the German by Martin Hardie.
Lugt, Frits.	*Les Marques de Collections de Dessins et d'Estampes.* Amsterdam, 1921.
Martial, Adolphe P.	*Nouveau Traité de la Graveur à l'Eau Forte.* Paris, 1873.
Paton, Hugh.	*Etching, Drypoint, and Mezzotint.* London, 1909.
,, ,,	*Colour Etching.* London, 1909.
Pennell, J.	*Etchers and Etching.* London, 1920.
,, ,,	*The Graphic Arts.* Chicago, 1921.
Plowman, G. T.	*Etching and other Graphic Arts.* London, 1915.
Prideaux, S. T.	*Aquatint Engraving.* London, 1909.
Profit, G.	*Procédés élémentaires de la gravure d'art Eau-forte.* Paris, 1913.
Reed, Earl H.	*Etching : a Practical Treatise.* New York, 1914.
Rensselaer, S. van.	*American Etchers.* New York, 1886.
Rhead, G. W.	*Etching* (Darton's Manuals). London, 1890.
Robert, Karl.	*Traité practique de la gravure à l'eau-forte.* Paris, 1891.
Salaman, Malcolm C.	*Modern Etchings, Mezzotints, and Drypoints.* Studio, Ltd. London, 1912.
,, ,,	*The Great Painter-Etchers from Rembrandt to Whistler.* Studio, Ltd. London, 1914.

Q

Salaman, Malcolm C.   *Graphic Arts of Great Britain.* Studio,
                        Ltd. London, 1917.

„   „   *The Charm of the Etcher's Art.* 3 folios.
                        Studio, Ltd. London, 1920.

„   „   *The Modern Adventure in Print Col-
                        lecting.* The Bookman's Journal,
                        Vol IV. 1921.

Salaman, Malcolm, C. and *Print Collectors' Handbook.* London,
  Whitman A.   1912.

Short, Sir Frank.   *On the Making of Etchings.* London,
                        1888.

„   „   *Etchings and Engravings.* London, 1911.

Short, Sir Frank, and   *A Descriptive Catalogue of a collection
  C. M. Pott.   of Tools and Materials used in Etching,*
                        exhibited in Victoria and Albert
                        Museum. London, 1910.

Shrubsole, W. G.   *Etching.* London [1889].

Sickert, Walter.   *Future of Engraving.*   Burlington
                        Magaznie, 1915, Vol. XXIII., p. 224.

„   „   *The Old Ladies of Etching-Needle Street.*
                        English Review, Jan. 1912.

Simpson, T.   *Modern Etchings and their Collectors.*
                        London, 1919.

Singer, H. W.   *Representative Art of our Time. Etching
                        and Drypoint.* The Studio. London.
                        1904.

„   „   *Die Moderne Graphik.* Leipzig, 1914.

Slater, J. H.   *Engravings and their Value.* London,
                        1921.

Smith, Sydney Ure.   *Art in Australia.* Sydney, 1921.

Stevens, Thomas Wood.   *The Etching of Cities.* Chicago Soc. of
                        Etchers, 1913.

Strang,   W.,   and   *Etching and Engraving.* London, 1897.
  Singer, H. W.

V. and A. Museum.   *Catalogue of Modern Etchings of the
                        Foreign Schools.* 1903.

„   „   *Catalogue of Etchings and Aquatints of
                        British and American Schools.* 1906.

Wedmore, Sir Frederick *Four Masters of Etching : Haden,
                        Jacquemart, Whistler, Legros.* London,
                        1883.

„   „   *Etching in England.* London, 1895.

„   „   *Fine Prints : a Study and Catalogue.*
                        London, 1910.

Wedmore, Sir Frederick.	*Etchings.* London, 1st ed., 1911; 2nd ed., 1912.
Weitenkampf, F.	*The Etchings of Contemporary Life.* Chicago, 1916.
Whitman, A.	*Print-Collectors' Handbook.* London, 1901.
Whitman, A., and Salaman, M. C.	*Print-Collectors' Handbook.* London, 1912.
Willshire, W. H.	*Introduction to the Study and Collection of Ancient Prints.* 2 vols. London, 1874.
Winslow, H.	*The Etching of Landscapes.* Chicago Soc. of Etchers, 1914.
Wray, Henry R.	*A Review of Etching in the United States.* Philadelphia, 1893.

Monographs on Artists and Catalogues of Their Work

AUSTEN, WINIFRED.
> Stokes, Hugh. *Art and Animals : The Etchings of Winifred Austen, R.E.* The Bookman's Journal and Print Collector, Vol. VI., No. 8, 1922.

BARYE, ANTOINE LOUIS.
> Delteil, Loys. *Barye.* Le Peintre Graveur Illustré, Vol. VI. Paris, 1910.

BEHAM, HANS SEBALD.
> Noseda, Mrs. *Catalogue of Prints and Etchings of H. S. Beham.* London, 1877.
> Pauli, G. *Hans Sebald Beham.* 2 vols. Strassburg, 1901.

BENSON, FRANK W.
> Paff, Adam E. M. *Etchings and Dry Points by Frank W. Benson.* 2 vols. Boston and New York, 1917 and 1919.

BESNARD, ALBERT.
> Coppier, A. C. *Les Eaux-Fortes de Besnard.* Paris, 1920.
> Janin, Clément. *Albert Besnard.* Print Coll. Quarterly, Vol. VIII., 1921.

BLAMPIED, E.
> Salaman, M. C. *Edmund Blamfield's Etchings.* The Bookman's Journal and Print Collector. Vol. VI., No. 11, 1922.

BONE, MUIRHEAD.
    Dodgson, Campbell. *Etching and Drypoints by Muirhead Bone.* London, 1909.
    Dodgson, Campbell. *The Late Dry-Points of Muirhead Bone.* Print Coll. Quarterly, Vol. IX., 1922.

BRACQUEMOND, FELIX.
    Weitenkampf, Frank. *Felix Bracquemond: An Etcher of Birds.* Print Coll. Quarterly, Vol. II., 1912.

BRANGWYN, FRANK.
    Newbolt, Frank. *Frank Brangwyn:* with catalogue of his etchings. London, 1908. 2nd ed., 1912.
    Sparrow, Walter Shaw. *Frank Brangwyn.* London, 1910.

BUHOT, FELIX.
    Bourcard, Gustave. *Felix Buhot.* Paris, 1899.

CALLOT, JACQUES.
    Green, J. H. *Callot. Catalogue and description of his Works.* London, 1804.
    Hellman, George S. *Jacques Callot.* Print Coll. Quarterly, Vol. IV., 1914.
    Meaume, Edouard. *Recherches sur la Vie et les Ouvrages de Jacques Callot.* Paris, 1860.
    Nasse, H. *Jacques Callot.* Leipzig [1909].
    Plan, P. P. *Jacques Callot, maître gravure.* Bruxelles, 1911.

CAMERON, D. Y.
    Wedmore, Sir F. *Cameron's Etchings: a Study and Catalogue.* London, 1903.
    Rinder, Frank. *Catalogue of the Etched Works of D. Y. Cameron.* Glasgow, 1912.

CANALE, ANTONIO.
    Metcalfe, Louis R. *Antonio Canale called Canaletto.* Print Coll. Quarterly, Vol. III., 1913.

CARPEAUX, J. B.
    Delteil, Loys. *Carpeaux.* Le Peintre Graveur Illustré, Vol. VI. Paris, 1910.

CASSATT, MARY.
    Weitenkamph, Frank. *The Dry Points of Mary Cassatt.* Print Coll. Quarterly, Vol. VI., 1916.

CLAUSEN, GEORGE.
    Gibson, Frank. *The Etchings of George Clausen, R.A.* Print Coll. Quarterly, Vol. VIII., 1921.

CONDER, CHARLES.
    Gibson, Frank. *Charles Conder. His Life and Work with Catalogue of Lithographs and Etchings,* by Campbell Dodgson. London, 1914.

COROT, J. B. C.
>Delteil, Loys. *Corot.* Le Peintre Graveur Illustré, Vol. V. Paris, 1910.
>
>Wickenden, R. J. *" Le Père Corot."* Print Coll. Quarterly, Vol. II., 1912.
>
>Wickenden, Robert J. *Le Père Corot.* Boston, 1914.

COTMAN, J. S.
>Popham, A. E. *The Etchings of John Sell Cotman.* Print Coll. Quarterly, Vol. IX., 1922.

CROME, JOHN.
>Theobald, H. S. *Crome's Etchings.* London, 1906.

CRUICKSHANK, GEORGE.
>Reid, G. W. *Catalogue of Works of George Cruickshank.* London, 1871.

DAUBIGNY, C. F.
>Delteil, Loys. *Daubigny.* Le Peintre Graveur Illustré, Vol. XIII., 1921.
>
>Wickenden, R. J. *C. F. Daubigny.* Print Coll. Quarterly, Vol. III., 1913.
>
>Wickenden, Robert J. *Charles François Daubigny : Painter and Etcher.* Boston, 1914.

DEGAS, H. G. E.
>Delteil, Loys. *Degas.* Le Peintre Graveur Illustré, Vol. IX. Paris, 1919.

DELACROIX, E.
>Delteil, Loys. *Delacroix.* Le Peintre Graveur Illustré, Vol. III. Paris, 1908.
>
>Moreau, Adolphe. *E. Delacroix et son œuvre.* Paris, 1873.
>
>Robaut, Alfred. *L'Œuvre Complet de Eugène Delacroix.* Paris, 1885.

DUPRÉ, JULES.
>Delteil, Loys. *Dupré.* Le Peintre Graveur Illustré, Vol. I. Paris, 1906.

DÜRER, ALBERT.
>Hind, A. M. *Albert Dürer.* The Great Engravers. London, 1911.
>
>Koehler, S. R. *Catalogue of Engravings, Dry Points and Etchings of Albert Dürer.* Grolier Club, New York, 1897.

EVERDINGEN, A. VAN.
>Drugulin, W. *Allart van Everdingen : Catalogue Raisonné.* Leipzig. 1873.

FITTON, HEDLEY.
>Dunthorne, Robert. *Catalogue of Etchings of Hedley Fitton, R.E.* London, 1911.

FORAIN, J. L.
> Dodgson, Campbell. *The Etchings of Jean Louis Forain.*
> Print Coll. Quarterly, Vol. VIII., 1921.
> Guérin, Marcel. *J. L. Forain. Catalogue de l'Œuvre Gravé de
> L'Artiste.* 2 vols. Paris, 1912.

FORBES, E. A.
> Sabin, A. K. *The Dry-Points of Elizabeth Adela Forbes.* Print
> Coll. Quarterly, Vol. IX., 1922.

GEDDES, A.
> Dodgson, Campbell. *Etchings of Andrew Geddes : Catalogue
> Raisonné.* Published by Walpole Society. Vol. V., 1919.
> Laing, David. *Etchings by Geddes and Wilkie.* Edinburgh,
> 1875.

GILLRAY, J.
> Grego, Joseph. *James Gillray.* London, n.d.

GOULDING, F.
> Hardie, Martin. *Frederick Goulding.* London, 1910.

GOYA, F. DE.
> Calvert, A. F. *Goya : an Account of his Life and Works.*
> London and New York, 1908.
> Hind, A. M. *Goya. The Great Engravers.* London, 1911.
> Hofmann, J. *Catalogue of Goya's Etched Work.* Vienna, 1907.
> Loga, Valerian von. *Francisco de Goya.* Berlin, 1903.
> Mather, F. J. jun. *Goya and " Los Desastres de La Guerra."*
> Print Coll. Quarterly, Vol. V., 1915.

GRIGGS, F. L.
> Malcolm C. Salaman. *The Etchings of F. L. Griggs, A.R.A.,
> R.E. (with Catalogue).* The Bookman's Journal and Print
> Collector, Vol. VII., No. 14, 1922.

HADEN, SIR F. SEYMOUR.
> Drake, Sir W. R. *Catalogue of Etched Work of Francis Sey-
> mour Haden.* London, 1880.
> Harrington, H. Nazeby. *A Supplement to Sir William Drake's
> Catalogue of the Etchings of Francis Seymour Haden.*
> London, 1903.
> Harrington, H. Nazeby. *Engraved Work of Sir Francis Sey-
> mour Haden.* London, 1910.
> Keppel, F. *Personal Characteristics of Sir Seymour Haden,
> P.R.E.* Print Coll. Quarterly, Vol. I., 1911.

HAIG, AXEL H.
> Armstrong, E. A. *Axel Herman Haig and his Work.* London,
> 1905.

HANKEY, W. LEE.
> Hardie, Martin. *The Etched Work of W. Lee-Hankey, R.E.*
> London [1921].

HERKOMER, SIR HUBERT.
> Baldry, A. L. *Hubert von Herkomer, R.A. : his Life and Work.*
> London, 1901.

HELLEU, PAUL.
> *A Gallery of Portraits from Etchings by P. Helleu.* London,
> 1907.

HOLLAR, W.
> Hind, A. M. *Wenceslaus Hollar and his Views of London and
> Windsor in the Seventeenth Century.* London, 1922.
> Parthey, G. *Wenzel Hollar.* Berlin, 1853. Supplement, 1858.
> Smith, Edward R. *Hollar's London.* Print Coll. Quarterly,
> Vol. V., 1915.
> Vertue, G. *Wenceslaus Hollar.* London, 1745.

HUET, PAUL.
> Delteil, Loys. *Paul Huet.* Le Peintre Graveur Illustré, Vol.
> VII. Paris, 1911.

INGRES, J. A. D.
> Delteil, Loys. *Ingres.* Le Peintre Graveur Illustré, Vol. III.
> Paris, 1908.

ISRAËLS, J.
> Hubert, H. J. *Etched Work of Josef Israëls.* Amsterdam,
> 1909.

JACQUE, C.
> Guiffrey, J. J. *Charles Jacque.* Paris, 1866.
> Wickenden, Robert J. *Charles Jacque.* Boston, 1914.
> Wickenden, R. J. *Charles Jacque.* Print Coll. Quarterly, Vol.
> II., 1912.

JACQUEMART, J.
> Gonse, Louis. *L'Œuvre de Jules Jacquemart.* Paris, 1876.
> Metcalfe, Louis R. *The Etchings of Jules Jacquemart.* Print
> Coll. Quarterly, Vol. VIII., 1921.

JOHN, A.
> Allhusen, E. L. *The Etched Work of Augustus John.* Print
> Coll. Quarterly, Vol. VII., 1917.
> Dodgson, Campbell. *Etchings by Augustus John.* London,
> 1920.

JONGKIND, JOAN BARTHOLD.
> Delteil, Loys. *Jongkind.* Le Peintre Graveur Illustré, Vol. I.
> Paris, 1906.

KLINGER, MAX.
  Singer, H. W. *Max Klinger's Radierungen Stiche*. Berlin,
    1909.

LALANNE, MAXIME.
  Bradley, W. A. *Maxime Lalanne*. Print Coll. Quarterly,
    Vol. III., 1913.
  Bradley, William Aspenwall. *Maxime Lalanne*. Boston, 1914.
LEGROS, A.
  Cary, Elizabeth, L. *Alphonse Legros*. Print Coll. Quarterly,
    Vol. II., 1912.
  Legros, L. A., and Wright, H. J. L. *Catalogue raisonné* (in
    preparation).
  Malassis, A. P. and Thibaudeau, A. W. *Catalogue raisonné de
    l'Œuvre gravé et lithographié d'Alphonse Legros*. Paris,
    1877.
LEHEUTRE, G.
  Delteil, Loys. *Gustave Leheutre*. Le Peintre Graveur Illustré,
    Vol. XII., 1921.
LEPÈRE, A.
  Bénédite, Léonce. *L'Œuvre Gravé de Auguste Lepère*. Paris
    [1906].
  Cary, Elizabeth. *Auguste Lepère*. Print Coll. Quarterly, Vol.
    II., 1912.
  Marx, Roger C. *Auguste Lepère*. Paris, 1919.
LHERMITTE, L.
  Henriet, Frederic. *Les Eaux-Fortes de Léon Lhermitte*. Paris,
    1905.
LIEBERMANN, MAX.
  Schiefler, Gustav. *Das Graphische Werk von Max Liebermann*.
    Berlin, 1907.
LUMSDEN, E. S.
  Salaman, M. C. *E. S. Lumsden, R.E.* Print Coll. Quarterly,
    Vol. VIII., 1921.
  Salaman, M. C. *Masterly Etchings by E. S. Lumsden, R.E.*
    The Bookman's Journal and Print Collector, Vol. VI.,
    No. 10, 1922.

McBEY, J.
  Salaman, M. C. *James McBey*. The Bookman's Journal and
    Print Collector, Vol. V., Nos. 1 and 2, 1921.
MACLAUGHLAN, D. S.
  Palmer, Cleveland. *The Recent Etchings of Donald Shaw
    Maclaughlan*. Print Coll. Quarterly, Vol. VI., 1916.

MANET, EDOUARD.
   Moreau-Nélaton, E. *Manet, Graveur et Lithographe.* Paris, 1906.
MEISSONIER, J. L. E.
   Schaus, William. *Etchings and Engravings by and after J. L. E. Meissonier.* New York [*c.* 1901].
MÉRYON, CHARLES.
   Bradley, W. A. *Charles Méryon, Poet.* Print Coll. Quarterly, Vol. III., 1913.
   Delteil, Loys. *Méryon.* Le Peintre Graveur Illustré, Vol. II. Paris, 1907.
   Dodgson, Campbell. *The Etchings of Charles Méryon.* The Studio, London, 1921.
   Huish, Marcus B. *Charles Méryon : a Memoir and complete descriptive Catalogue of his Works.* From the French of Philip Burty. London, 1879.
   Stokes, Hugh. *Etchings of Charles Méryon.* (Great Etchers Series.) London : Newnes, 1906.
   Stokes, Hugh. *Meryon and Paris : New Sidelights.* The Bookman's Journal and Print Collector, Vol. V., No. 2, 1921.
   Wedmore, Sir F. *Méryon and Méryon's Paris.* London, 1st ed., 1879; 2nd ed., 1892.
   Wright, Harold J. L. *Some undescribed states of Méryon Etchings.* Print Coll. Quarterly, Vol. VIII., 1921.
MILLET, J. F.
   Delteil, Loys. *Millet.* Le Peintre Graveur Illustré, Vol. I. Paris, 1906.
   Wickenden, R. J. *Jean François Millet.* Print Coll. Quarterly, Vol. II., 1912.
   Wickenden, Robert J. *The Art and Etchings of Jean-François Millet.* Boston, 1914.

PALMER, S.
   Hardie, Martin. *Catalogue of Samuel Palmer's Etchings.* Print Coll. Quarterly, Vol. III., No. 2, p. 225.
   Palmer, A. H. *Life and Letters of Samuel Palmer.* London, 1891.
PIRANESI, G. B.
   Focillon, Henri. *G. B. Piranesi : Essai de Catalogue de son Œuvre.* Paris, 1918.
   Giesecke, A. *Giovanni Battista Piranesi.* Leipzig, 1911.
   Hind, A. M. *Giovanni Battista Piranesi : a Critical Study.* London, 1922.

PIRANESI, G. B. (*cont.*)

Ivins, W. M. jun. *Piranesi and " Le Carceri D'Invenzione."* Print Coll. Quarterly, Vol. V., 1915.

Moore, Benjamin B. *G. B. Piranesi.* Print Coll. Quarterly, Vol. II., 1912.

Samuel. A. *G. Piranesi.* London, 1910.

PISSARRO, C.

Rodo, Ludovic. *The Etchings of Camille Pissarro.* Print Coll. Quarterly, Vol. IX., 1922.

RAJON, P. A.

Wickenden, R. J. *Paul Adolphe Rajon.* Print Coll. Quarterly, Vol. VI., 1916.

REDON, ODILON.

Mellerio, André. *Odilon Redon : Catalogue de l'Œuvre Gravé.* Paris, 1913.

REMBRANDT.

Bartsch, Adam. *Catalogue raisonné de toutes les estampes qui forment l'œuvre de Rembrandt.* Vienna, 1797.

Binyon, Laurence. *Rembrandt's Landscape Etchings.* Print Coll. Quarterly, Vol. II., 1912.

Blanc, Charles. *L'Œuvre Complet de Rembrandt.* 2 vols. Paris, 1873; 2nd ed., 1880.

Claussin, J. J. de. *Catalogue raisonné de toutes les estampes qui forment l'œuvre de Rembrandt.* Paris, 1824; 2nd ed., 1828.

Coppier, A. C. *Les Eaux-Fortes de Rembrandt.* Paris, 1917.

Daulby, Daniel. *Descriptive Catalogue of Works of Rembrandt, Bol, Lievens, and Van Vliet.* London, 1796.

Dutuit, Eugène. *L'Œuvre Complet de Rembrandt.* 3 vols. Paris, 1881–1884.

Gersaint, Edme F. *Catalogue raisonné l'œuvre de Rembrandt,* 1751. English translation, 1752.

Haden, Sir F. Seymour, P.R.E. *The Etched Work of Rembrandt.* London, 1879.

Hamerton, P. G. *The Etchings of Rembrandt.* Portfolio monograph. London, 1894.

Hind, A. M. *Etchings of Rembrandt.* Great Etchers Series. London : G. Newnes. Great Engravers Series. London : Heinemann. 1912.

Hind, A. M. *Rembrandt's Etchings.* 2 vols. London, 1912.

Holmes, Sir C. J. *Notes on the Art of Rembrandt.* London, 1911.

Holmes, Sir C. J. *The Development of Rembrandt as an Etcher.* Burlington Magazine. Vol. ix. 1906. London.

REMBRANDT (*cont.*)

Knackfuss, H. *Rembrandt.* Translated by Campbell Dodgson. Bielefeld, 1899.

Middleton-Wake, C. H. *Catalogue of the Etched Work of Rembrandt.* London, 1878.

Rovinski, D. *L'Œuvre gravé de Rembrandt.* Text (1 vol.), plates (3 vols.). St. Petersburg, 1890.

Rovinski, D. *L'Œuvre gravé des élèves de Rembrandt et des maîtres qui ont gravé dans son goût.* St. Petersburg, 1894.

Seidlitz, Woldemar von. *Kritisches Verzeichnis der Radierungen Rembrandt's.* Leipzig, 1895.

Singer, H. W. *Rembrandt's Radierungen.* Stuttgart, 1906.

Wedmore, Sir F. *Rembrandt : His Life and Work by E. Michel.* London, 1894.

Wilson, T. *Descriptive Catalogue of the Prints of Rembrandt.* London, 1836.

RENOUARD, P.

Janin, Cléments. *Paul Renouard.* Print Coll. Quarterly, Vol. IX., 1922.

RICHTER, A. L.

Singer, H. W. *Kritische Verzeichnis der Radierungen von A. L. Richter.* Dresden, 1913.

ROBINS, W. P.

Salaman, M. C. *The Etchings and Dry-Points of W. P. Robins.* The Bookman's Journal and Print Collector, Vol. V., No. 4, 1921.

ROBINSON, SIR J. C.

Allhusen, E. L. *Sir J. C. Robinson's Etchings.* Print Coll. Quarterly, Vol. VIII., 1921.

RODIN, AUGUSTE.

Delteil, Loys. *Rodin.* Le Peintre Graveur Illustré, Vol. VI. Paris, 1910.

ROPS, F.

Ramiro, Erastène. *Catalogue de Félicien Rops.* Bruxelles, 1893.

Mascha, Dr. Ottokar. *Félicien Rops.* Munich, 1910.

ROTH, E. D.

Mather, T. J., jun. *Etchings of Ernest D. Roth.* Print Coll. Quarterly, Vol. I., 1911.

ROUSSEAU, TH.

Delteil, Loys. *Rousseau.* Le Peintre Graveur Illustré, Vol. I. Paris, 1906.

ROWLANDSON, T.

Grego, Joseph. *Rowlandson, the Caricaturist.* 2 vols. London, 1880.

RUYSDAEL, J.
    Bradley, W. A. *Etchings of Jacob Ruysdael.* Print Coll.
        Quarterly, Vol. VII., 1917.

SHERBORN, C. W.
    Hopson, W. F. *C. W. Sherborn : an Appreciation.* 1910.
    Sherborn, C. D. *Sketch of the Life and Work of C. W. Sherborn.*
        London, 1912.
SHORT, SIR FRANK.
    Salaman, M. C. *Sir Frank Short, R.A., P.R.E., Master Engraver.*
        The Bookman's Journal and Print Collector, Vol. V.,
        No. 6, 1921.
    Strange, E. F. *The Etched and Engraved Work of Frank
        Short, R.A.* London, 1908.
SMILLIE, J. D.
    Smillie, James D. *Some Work by James D. Smillie.* The
        Century Assoc. New York, 1910.
SMITH, J. A.
    Laurvik, J. Nilsen. *J. André Smith.* Print Coll. Quarterly,
        Vol. IV., 1914.
SMITH, PERCY.
    Dodgson, Campbell. *Mr. Percy Smith's " Dance of Death."*
        Print Coll. Quarterly, Vol. VIII., 1921.
STAUFFER-BERN, KARL.
    Lehrs, Max. *Karl Stauffer-Bern,* 1857–1891. Dresden, 1907.
STEINLEN, A. T.
    Crauzat, E. de. *L'Œuvre de Steinlen.* Paris, 1913.
STRANG, IAN.
    Etchings and Dry-Points by Ian Strang. London, 1920.
STRANG, W.
    Binyon, Laurence. *The Etchings and Engravings of William
        Strang.* Print Coll. Quarterly, Vol. VIII., 1921.
    Catalogue of Etchings, with Introduction by Laurence Binyon.
        Glasgow, 1906.
    Catalogue of Etched Works, 1906–1912. Glasgow, 1912.
STRUCK, H.
    Schwarz, C. *Das Graphische Werk von Hermann Struck.*
        Berlin, 1911.

TIEPOLO, G. B.
    Hind, A. M. *The Etchings of G. B. Tiepolo.* Print Coll.
        Quarterly, Vol. VIII., 1921.
    Molmenti, Pompeo. *Acque-Forti dei Tiepolo.* Venice, 1896.

TOULOUSE-LAUTREC, HENRI DE.
> Delteil, Loys. *Toulouse-Lautrec.* Le Peintre Graveur Illustré, Vol. X. (1). Paris, 1920.

TURNER, J. M. W.
> Rawlinson, W. G. *Descriptive Catalogue of Turner's Liber Studiorum.* London, 1878; 2nd ed., 1906.

TUSHINGHAM, S.
> Konody, P. G. *Etchings and Dry-Points by S. Tushingham.* London [1922].

VAN DYCK, A.
> Carpenter, W. H. *Vandyck's Etchings.* London, 1844.
> Hind, A. M. *Van Dyck.* The Great Engravers. London, 1911.
> Hind, A. M. *Van Dyck : his Original Etchings and his Iconography.* Boston and New York, 1915.
> Hind, A. M. *Vandyck : his Original Etchings.* Print Coll. Quarterly, Vol. V., 1915.
> Wibiral, Dr. Franz. *L'Iconographie d'Antoine Van Dyck.* Leipzig, 1877.

VELDE, VAN DE.
> Bradley, W. A. *The Van de Veldes.* Print Coll. Quarterly, Vol. VII., 1917.
> Franken, D., and P. Van der Kellen. *L'Œuvre de Jan Van de Velde.* Amsterdam and Paris, 1883.

VIERGE, D.
> Marthold, Jules de. *Daniel Vierge.* Paris [1907].

WALCOT, W.
> Salaman, M. C. *William Walcot and his Roman Compositions.* The Bookman's Journal and Print Collector, Vol. V., No. 3, 1921.

WATTEAU, A.
> Hind, A. M. *Watteau . . . and French Engravers and Etchers.* The Great Engravers. London, 1911.

WEBSTER, HERMAN A.
> Hardie, Martin. *Herman A. Webster.* Print Coll. Quarterly, Vol. II., 1912.

WHISTLER, J. McN.
> Dodgson, Campbell. *Two unpublished Whistlers.* Print Coll. Quarterly, Vol. VII., 1917.
> Dodgson, Campbell. *The Etchings of J. McN. Whistler.* The Studio, London, 1922.
> Kennedy, E. G. *The Etched Work of Whistler.* Grolier Club Catalogue. With 3 portfolios containing over 1000 reproductions. New York, 1910.

WHISTLER, J. McN. (*cont.*)

    Mansfield, Howard. *Whistler.* Chicago, 1909.

       ,,   ,,   *Whistler as a Critic of his own Prints.*
    Print Coll. Quarterly, Vol. III., 1913.

    Mansfield, Howard. *Whistler in Belgium and Holland.* Print
    Coll. Quarterly, Vol. VI., 1916.

    Menpes, Mortimer. "*Whistler as I knew him.*" London, 1904.

    Pennell, E. R. and J. *The Life of James McN. Whistler.*
    2 vols. London and Philadelphia, 1908.

    Smith, John Russell. *A Catalogue of the Etchings and Dry-
    Points of J. A. McN. Whistler.* London, 1874.

    Wedmore, Sir F. *Whistler's Etchings : a Study and Catalogue.*
    London, 1st ed., 1886; 2nd ed., 1899.

WILKIE, DAVID.

    Laing, David. *Etchings by Wilkie and Geddes.* Edinburgh,
    1875.

ZILCKEN, P.

    Pit, A. *Catalogue descriptif des eaux fortes de Ph. Zilcken.*
    Amsterdam, 1918.

ZORN, A.

    Delteil, Loys. *Zorn.* Le Peintre Graveur Illustré, Vol. IV.
    Paris, 1909.

    Asplund, Dr. Karl. *Anders Zorn : his Life and Work.*
    "Studio" Office, 1921.

    —— *The Etched Work of Anders Zorn.* 2 vols. Stockholm,
    1920.

GENERAL CATALOGUES.

    Andresen, Andreas. *Der Deutsche Peintre-graveur.* 5 vols.
    Leipzig, 1864–1878.

    Bartsch, Adam. *Le Peintre Graveur.* 21 vols. Vienna, 1803–
    1821. Reprinted 1920.

    Béraldi, Henri. *Les Graveurs du Dix-neuvième Siècle.* 12 vols.
    Paris, 1885–1892.

    Dumesnil, Robert. *Le Peintre-graveur Français.* 11 vols.
    Paris, 1835–1871.

    Dutuit, Eugène. *Manuel de l'Amateur d'Estampes.* 6 vols.
    Paris, 1884–1885.

    Le Blanc, C. *Manuel de l'Amateur d'Estampes.* 4 vols.
    Paris, 1854.

    Vesme, A. de. *Le Peintre-graveur Italien.* Milan, 1906.

INDEX

A

Altdorfer, Albrecht, 44
Amman, Jost, 44
Ammonia, use of, 21
Appian, Adolphe, 145
Aquatint; Biting, 193–194
—— Charcoal, use of, 20
—— Dust-grounds, 187, 189
—— Famous examples, 197–198
—— History of, 185–186
—— Sand-paper, 187, 198–199
—— Spirit-grounds, 188, 194
—— Technique of, 187–197

B

Backhuysen, Ludolf, 66, 79, 81
Barocci of Urbino, 47
Bartsch, Adam, 70
Bath, Nitric, 27, 28
—— Dutch, 29
—— Perchloride of Iron, 30
Bauer, Marius, 151, 156
Bega, Cornelius, 66, 73, 75
Beham, Hans Sebald, 44
Bella, Stefano Della, 47
Berchem, Nicolaes, 66, 69
Bevel of Plate, 21
Bibliography of Works on Etching and Etchers, 222–238
Biting the plate, 27
—— Aquatint, 193–194
—— Foul, 31, 32, 35, 38
—— Re-biting, 32
Blampied, E., 127
Blankets for printing, 210, 211
Bol, Ferdinand, 66
Bone, Muirhead, 4, 12, 174, 175, 177–179, 218

Bosse, Abraham, 10, 15, 22 55
Both, Jan, 66, 69
Bracquemond, Felix, 11, 109, 134, 140, 141
Brangwyn, Frank, 4, 114, 121
British Museum, 44, 62, 91, 198, 200, 218
British School of Etching, origin of, 80
Brockhurst, G., 127
Bur (drypoint) 18, 159, 163–164
Burdett, Paul, 186
Burgkmair, Hans (Younger), 44
Burin, 16, 17, 18
Burnisher, 16, 17, 36, 37, 38
Burridge, F., 127
Buytenwegh, William, 48

C

Callipers, use of, 37
Callot, Jacques, 10, 48, 52, 53
Cameron, D. Y., 12, 113, 116, 176, 180, 181
Canale, G. A. (Canaletto), 11, 85, 90
Care of prints, 213–214
Castiglione, 47
Charcoal, 17, 20
Chinese white, 25
Chloroform, use of, 25
Claude (*see* Gellée).
Clausen, George, 117, 118, 121, 218
Cleaning the plate, 21
Constable, 79
Continental etchers, nineteenth and twentieth centuries, 127–156
Copper, 20
Corot, Jean Baptiste Camille, 132, 134
Cotman, John Sell, 91, 202, 203
Counterproofs, 212
Crocus powder, use of, 16, 19
Crome, John, 11, 79, 91, 94, 201, 203

Printed in Great Britain by Richard Clay & Sons, Limited,
BUNGAY, SUFFOLK.

P. & D. COLNAGHI & CO.

ESTABLISHED 1760

Paintings, Drawings, Engravings and Etchings
By the
Old and Modern Masters

Publishers of Original Etchings and Drypoints
By
Muirhead Bone, James McBey,
E. S. Lumsden, W. P. Robins,
Etc., Etc.

Galleries :
144, 145, 146, New Bond Street,
London, W. 1

Telegrams:
Colnaghi, Wesdo, London.

Telephone:
Mayfair 6356 (3 lines)

ETCHING PRESSES

and

Etching Materials of every
description

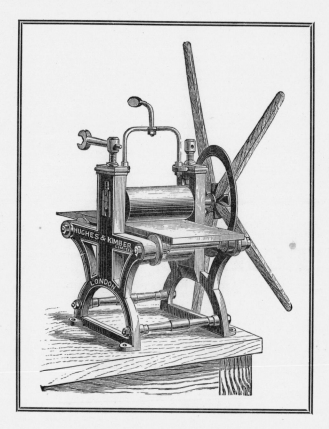

:: *can be obtained at* ::

HUGHES & KIMBER,

9 Gough Square, London, E.C. 4.

ESTABLISHED 1820.